D0236087

1000 WORDS STEM

Jules Pottle

DK

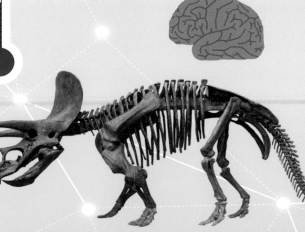

DK | Penguin Random House

Written by Jules Pottle
Editors Sophie Parkes, Robin Moul
Senior Editors James Mitchem, Dawn Sirett
Designers Rachael Hare, Sadie Thomas
Managing Editor Penny Smith
Managing Art Editor Mabel Chan
Art Director Helen Senior
Publishing Director Sarah Larter
Production Editor Abi Maxwell
Production Controller Inderjit Bhullar

First published in Great Britain in 2021 by
Dorling Kindersley Limited
DK, One Embassy Gardens, 8 Viaduct Gardens,
London, SW11 7BW

Imported into the EEA by Dorling Kindersley Verlag GmbH.
Arnulfstr. 124, 80636 Munich, Germany

A CIP catalogue record for this book
is available from the British Library.
ISBN: 978-0-2414-5896-9
Printed and bound in China

www.dk.com

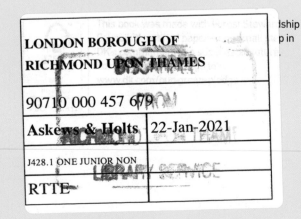

1000 WORDS
STEM

A note for parents about STEM...

STEM subjects are those which incorporate science, technology, engineering, and maths. They often overlap. You need mathematical measurements to collect the results from a science experiment. You need to write computer programs to operate the machines you have engineered. You need to understand the science of forces to be a structural engineer. STEM subjects are highly interlinked and many of the words from one subject will be useful when learning about another.

Children will meet a lot of new words when they begin to study STEM subjects at school. A great deal of technical vocabulary is used in these lessons: names for pieces of equipment, names for things we cannot see (such as forces), and words that describe a specific property of materials (such as "opaque"). These may all be new to children.

This book contains topics and words that children are likely to encounter in their first few years at school. It also includes many of the topics that fascinate children in this age group, and some that show how STEM subjects are present in our everyday lives.

A broad vocabulary can help children to access their education more easily. Spending time with children and talking about the words and the illustrations in this book will expose them to more than just the words written here, as they will encounter additional words as part of the conversation. This book is a great place to start your child's STEM education.

Jules Pottle, primary science consultant, teacher, and trainer

Contents

Hot and cold

How warm are you right now? Some places in the world are warm while others are freezing cold.

sunglasses

fireworks

summer

hot

Sun

orang-utan

fire

explode

bonfire

Equator

lizard

desert

sand

coat

flask

camel

icicles

hot
water
bottle

cactus

ice
cubes

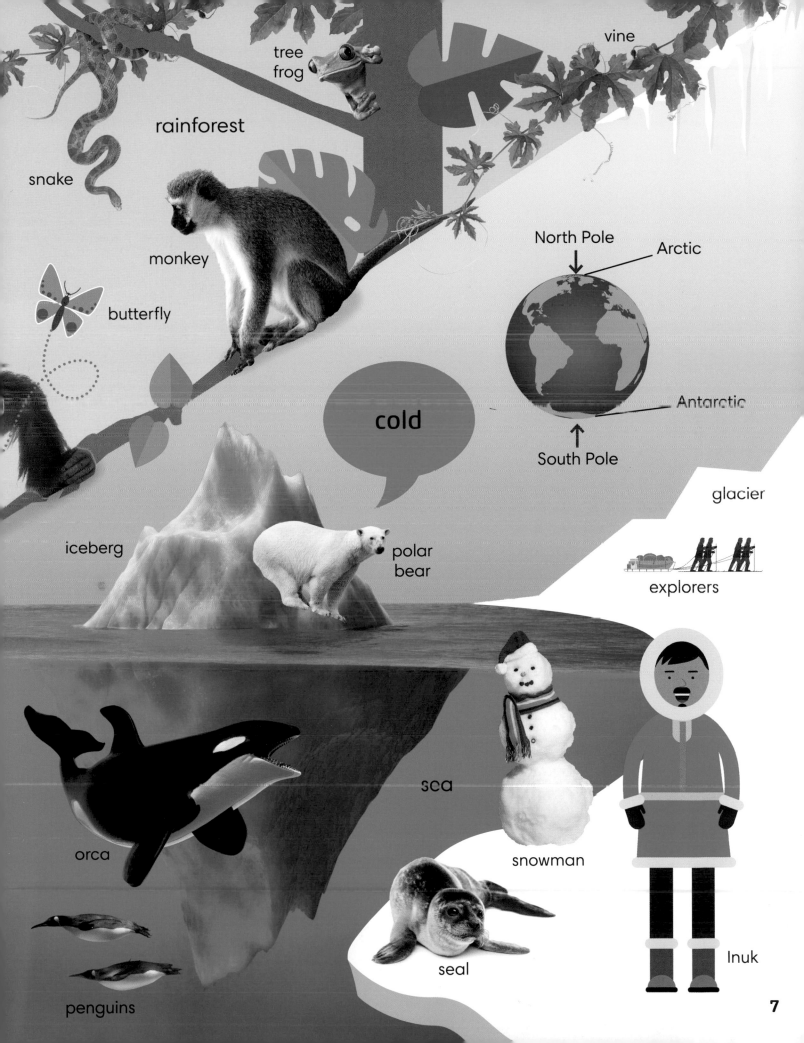

vine

tree frog

rainforest

snake

monkey

butterfly

North Pole

Arctic

Antarctic

South Pole

cold

glacier

iceberg

polar bear

explorers

orca

sea

snowman

seal

Inuk

penguins

7

Seasons

As the Earth orbits the Sun, countries near the North and South Poles move through different seasons. Winter is usually cold. In spring, the weather gets warmer. It is hottest in summer, and then cools down again in autumn.

cold

snowflake

Christmas lights

reindeer

evergreen tree

changing colour

fireworks

fog

rain

umbrella

ice skates

snow

waterproof

wet

bonfire

candles

wellies

falling

Diwali lamp

puddle

Hanukkah lights

leaves

autumn

winter

bird

eggs

nest

sky

beach

fruit

warm

blossom

harvest

shade

hot

calf

lamb

sheep

butterfly

cow

tadpoles

bee

water

watering
can

rabbit

baby
rabbit

sunhat

pollen

sun
cream

cool box

flower

shoot

caterpillar

spring

frog

summer

9

Sound

The world around us is bursting with different noises. Do you know what all of these sound like?

beat

strings

tap

pluck

rhythm

shake

rattle

instrument

music

guitar

sound waves

traffic

ear

whisper

laugh

hearing aid

talk

silence

deaf

hear

ear bone

listen

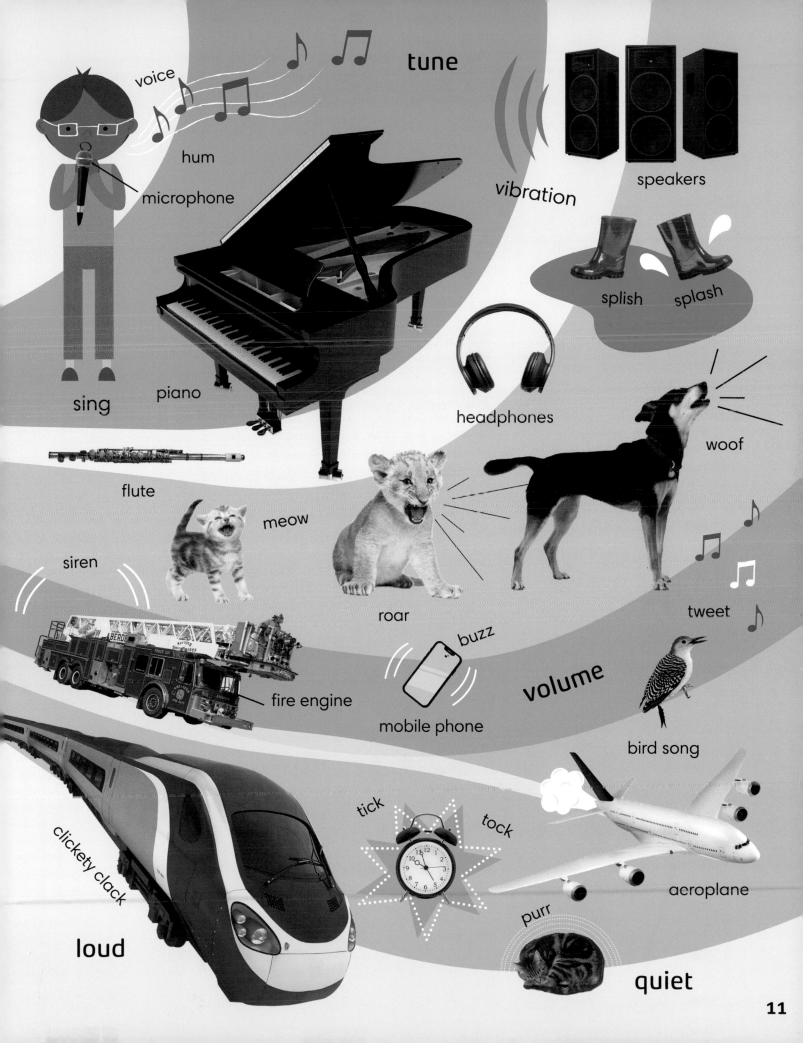

voice

tune

hum

microphone

speakers

vibration

splish   splash

piano

sing

headphones

woof

flute

meow

roar

siren

tweet

fire engine

buzz

mobile phone

bird song

volume

clickety clack

tick

tock

aeroplane

purr

loud

quiet

11

Machines

We build machines to help us. They can be small and simple or big and complicated.

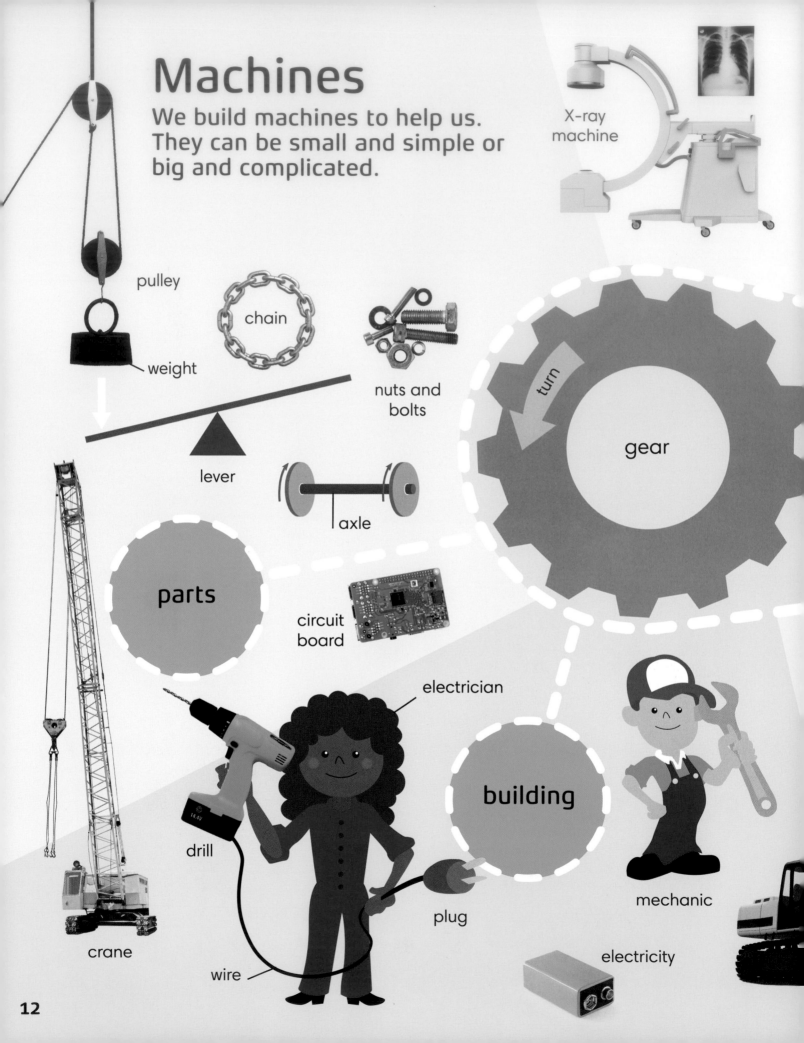

X-ray machine

pulley

weight

chain

nuts and bolts

lever

axle

turn

gear

parts

circuit board

electrician

crane

drill

building

mechanic

wire

plug

electricity

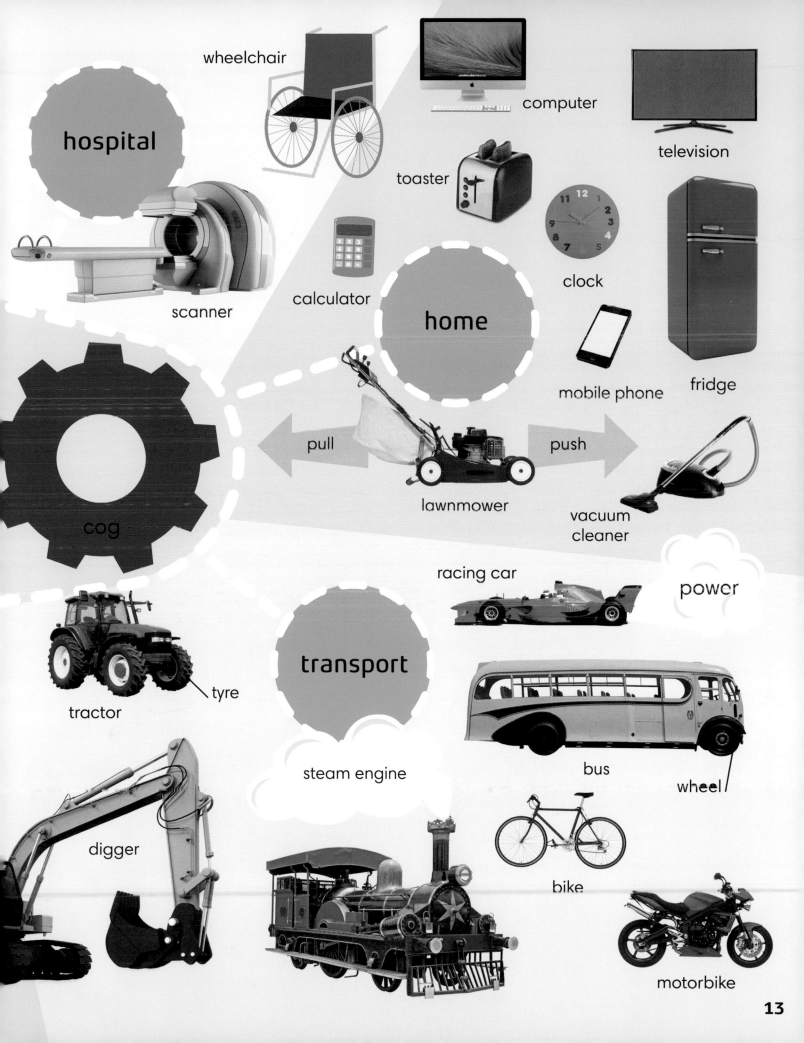

hospital

wheelchair

computer

television

scanner

toaster

clock

fridge

calculator

home

mobile phone

cog

pull

push

lawnmower

vacuum cleaner

racing car

power

tyre

transport

bus

tractor

steam engine

wheel

digger

bike

motorbike

Space

Have you ever looked at the night sky and wondered what's out there, in space?

shooting star

star

black

outer space

Cassiopeia constellation

asteroid

Solar System

Mars

light

Sun

day

night

Earth

Venus

Mercury

Jupiter

solar panel

satellite

Mars Rover

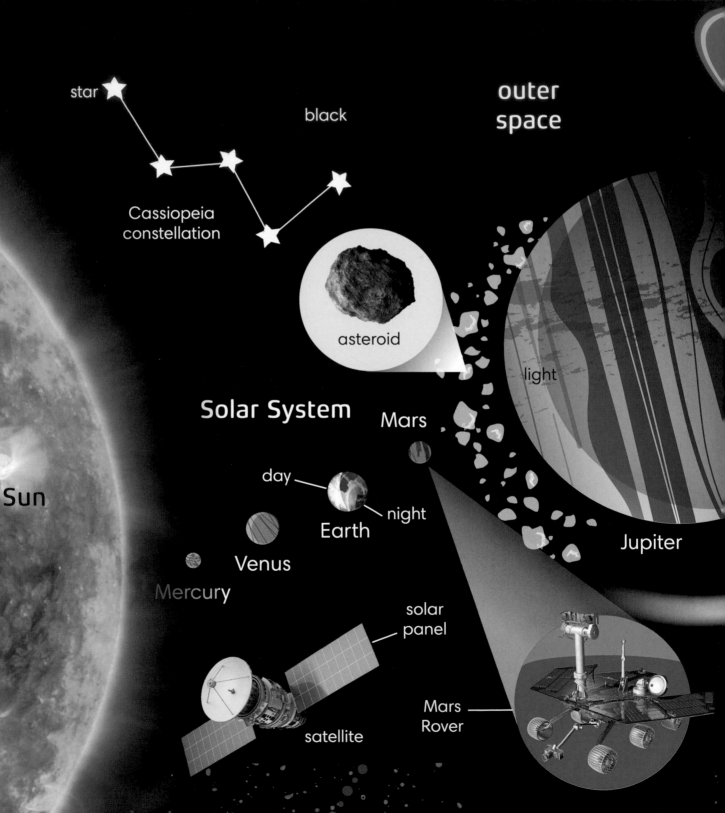

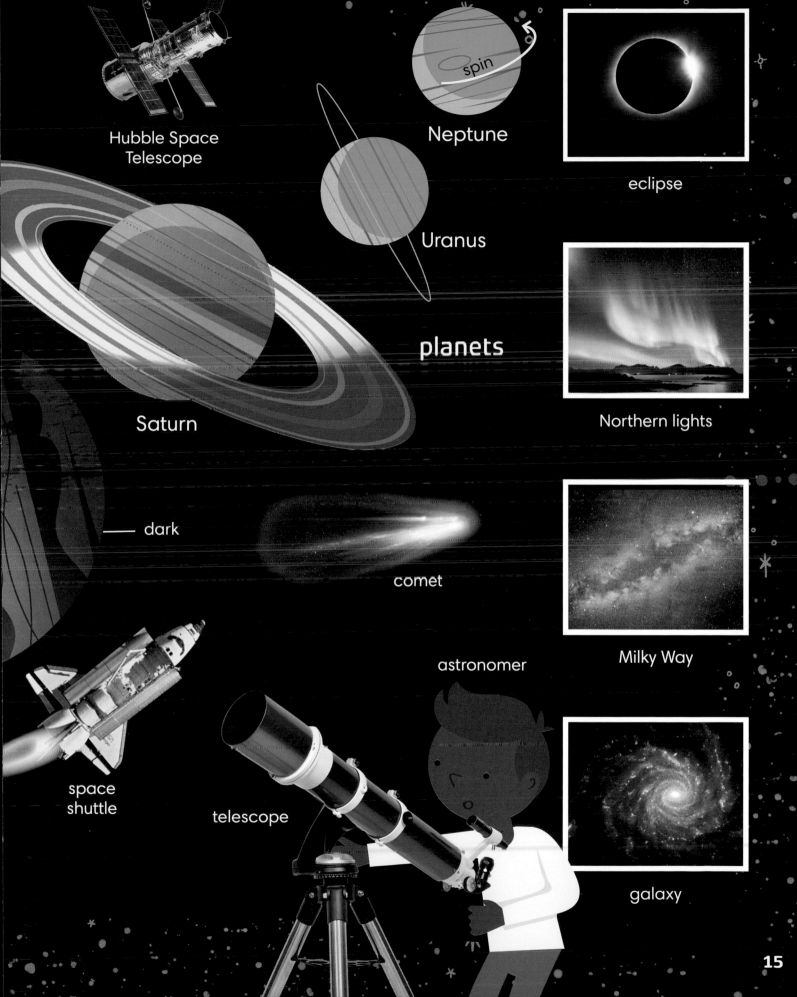

Hubble Space
Telescope

Neptune

spin

eclipse

Uranus

planets

Northern lights

Saturn

dark

comet

Milky Way

astronomer

space
shuttle

telescope

galaxy

Moon landing

What do you think it would be like to be an astronaut like Neil and Buzz, the first people to walk on the Moon?

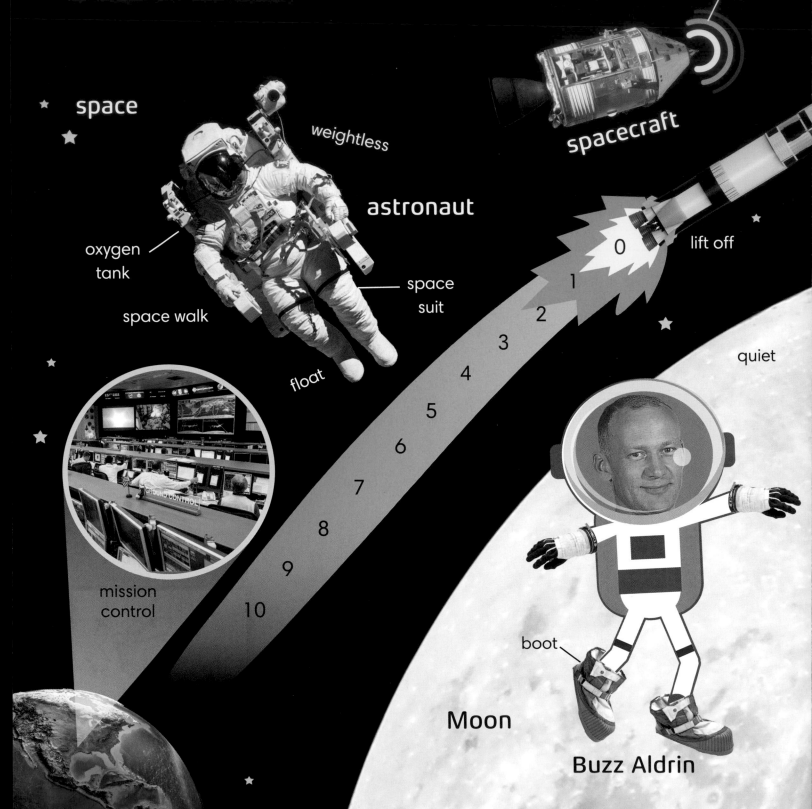

radio

space

weightless

spacecraft

astronaut

oxygen tank

lift off

0

1

2

3

4

5

6

7

8

9

10

space suit

space walk

float

quiet

mission control

boot

Moon

Buzz Aldrin

Transport

There are lots of ways to travel. How many of these types of transport have you used?

funicular railway

beep

horn

4x4 jeep

pick-up truck

coach

soft top

monster truck

indicator

lorry

quad bike

petrol station

charger

electric car

taxi

steam engine

engine

bullet train

road

tram

underground train

tracks

underground

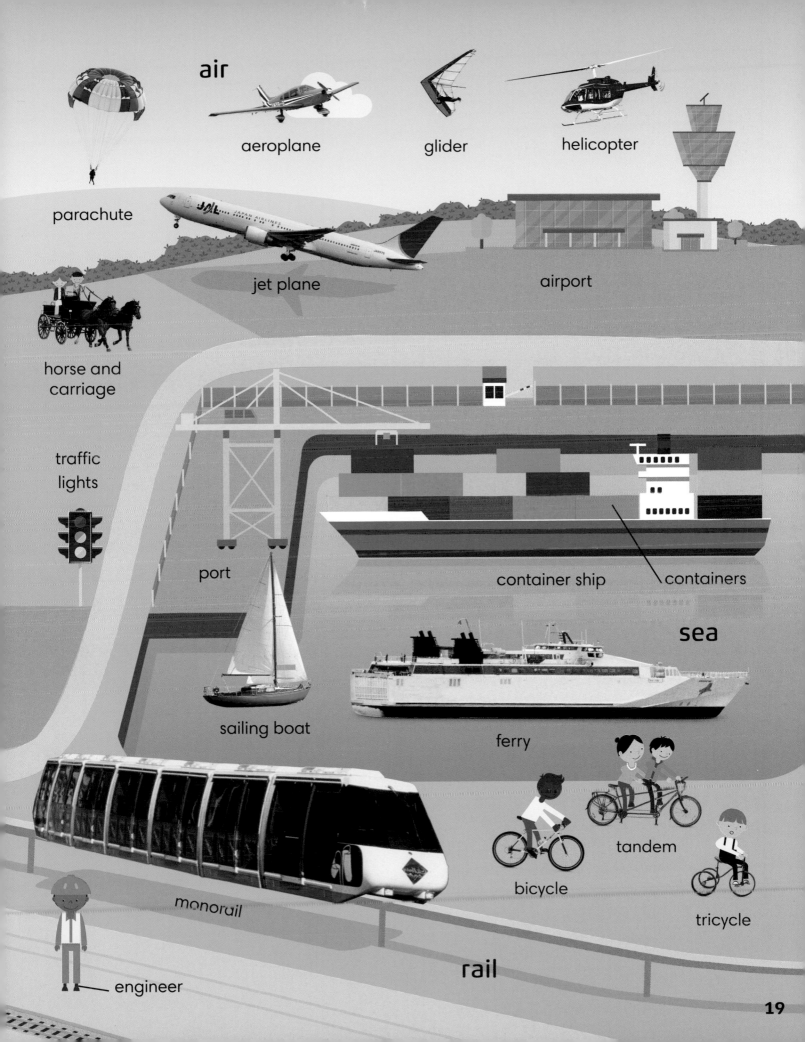

air

parachute

aeroplane

glider

helicopter

jet plane

airport

horse and carriage

traffic lights

port

container ship

containers

sea

sailing boat

ferry

monorail

bicycle

tandem

tricycle

engineer

rail

19

Vehicles

Many machines are designed to move people and things around. We call them vehicles.

aerodynamic

fighter jet

lifeboat

speedboat

ship

submarine

army truck

tank

dump truck

cab

backhoe loader

bulldozer

caterpillar tracks

excavator

drone

horse box

combine harvester

tractor

baler

flag

tyre

spoiler

streamlined

pit stop

racing car

grip

motorbike

wheel

ramp

siren

ambulance

police car

fire engine

garage

crane

jack

car lift

mechanic

Weather

What is the weather like today? It can change from season to season or from day to day. In some places, it can even change several times in one day!

rainbow

blue sky

Sun

bright

light

hot

humid

wind

windmill

sweaty

frozen

wind turbine

tornado

dry

thunder

cloud

storm cloud

hail

storm

rain

raindrops

lightning

colours

showers

mist

drizzle

snow

wet

cold

snowstorm

damp

ice crystal

chilly

forecast

23

At the doctor's

The doctor can work out what is wrong with us and help us to get better when we are poorly.

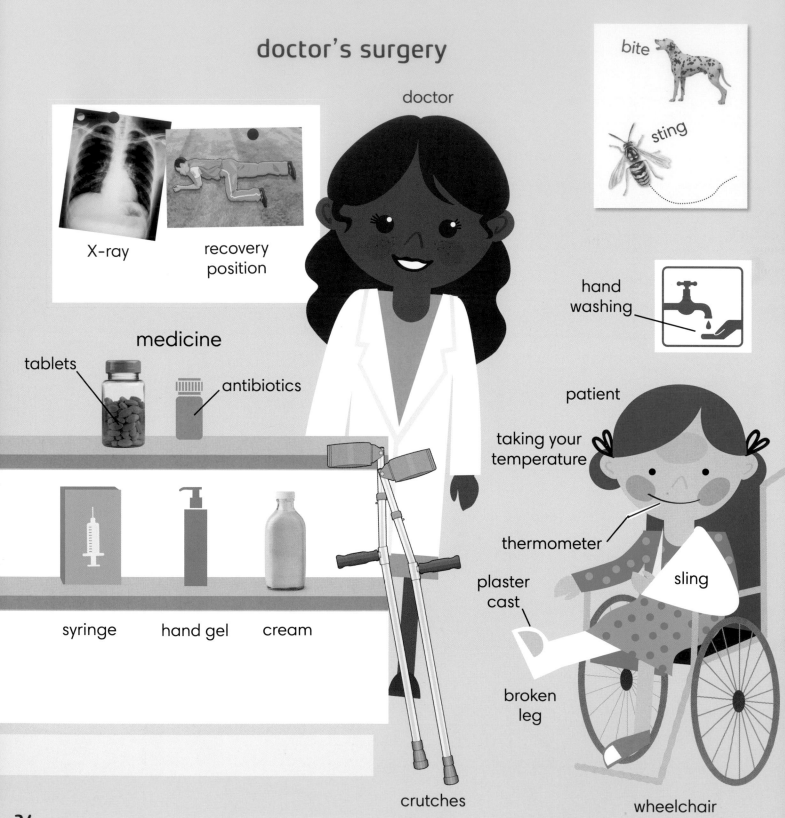

doctor's surgery

bite

sting

doctor

X-ray

recovery position

hand washing

medicine

tablets

antibiotics

patient

taking your temperature

thermometer

plaster cast

sling

broken leg

syringe

hand gel

cream

crutches

wheelchair

24

germs

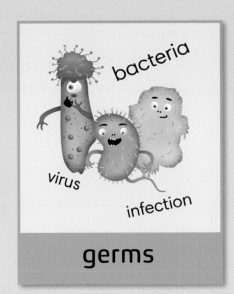

bacteria

virus

infection

hospital

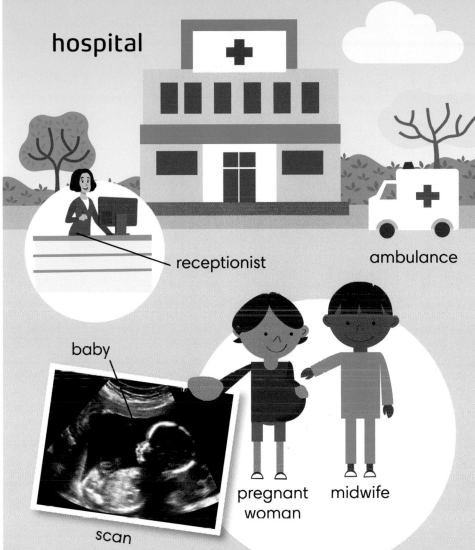

receptionist

ambulance

baby

scan

pregnant woman

midwife

weighing scales

height chart

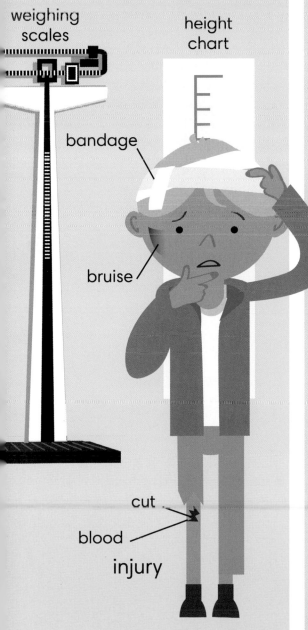

bandage

bruise

cut

blood

injury

operation

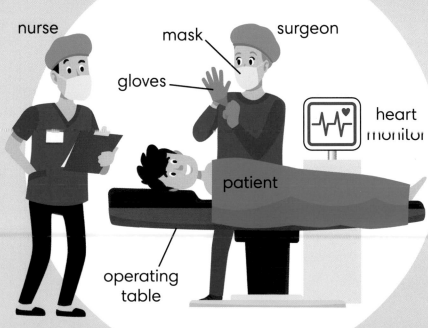

nurse

mask

surgeon

gloves

heart monitor

patient

operating table

Human body

Your body is amazing! It has so many parts, and it can do so many wonderful things!

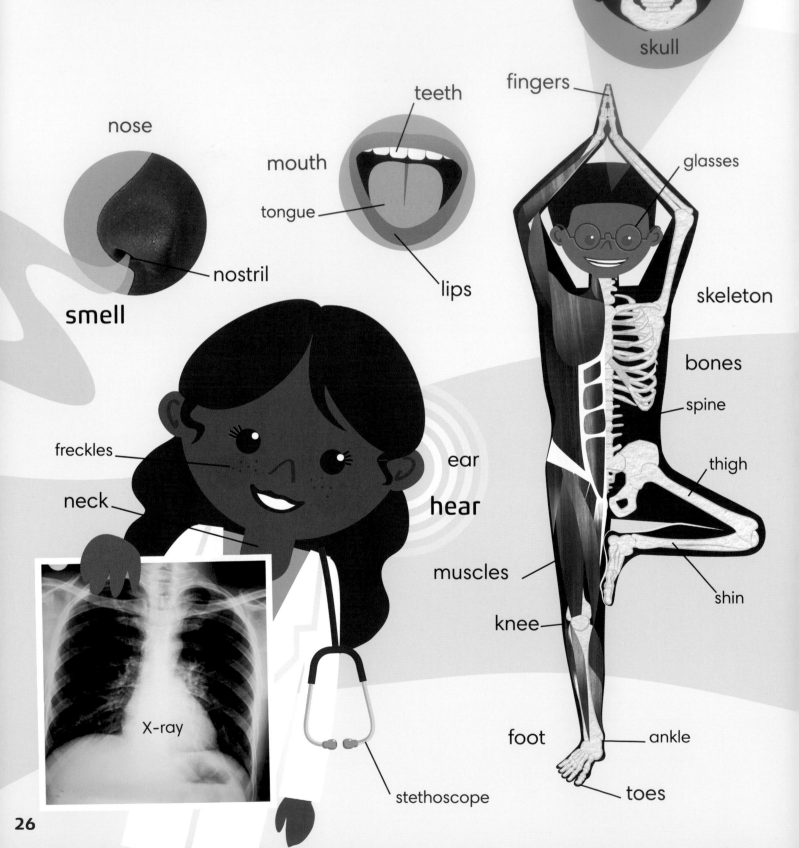

skull

nose

smell

nostril

teeth

mouth

tongue

lips

fingers

glasses

skeleton

bones

spine

thigh

ear

hear

freckles

neck

muscles

knee

shin

X-ray

stethoscope

foot

ankle

toes

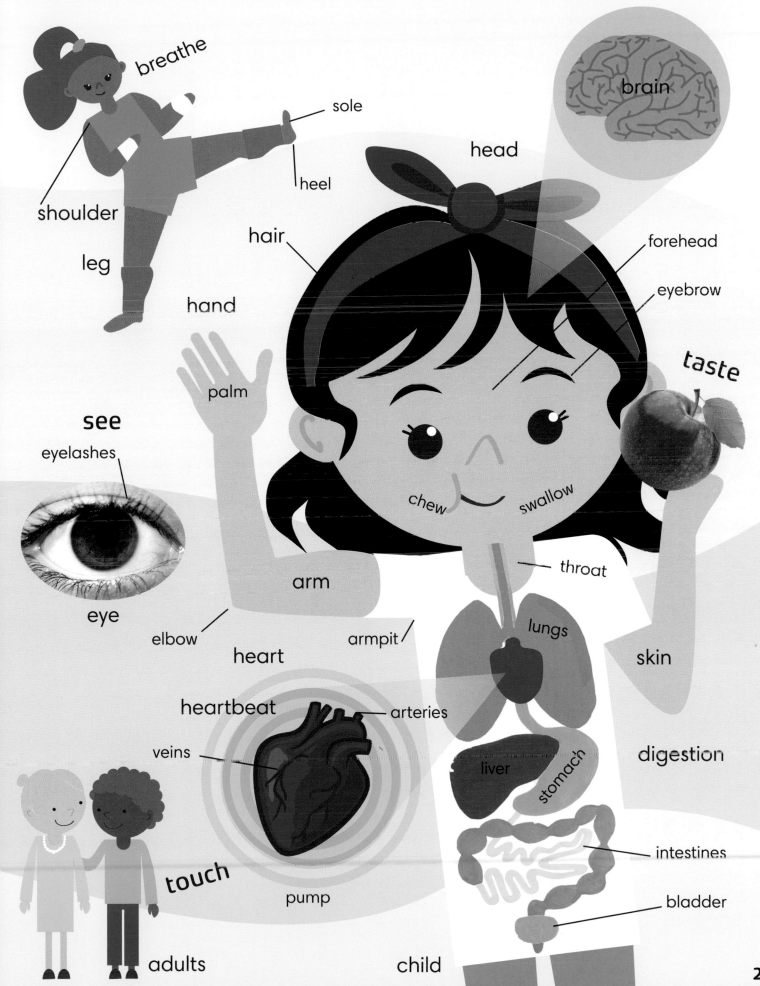

breathe

sole

heel

shoulder

leg

brain

head

hair

forehead

eyebrow

hand

taste

palm

see

eyelashes

chew

swallow

eye

throat

arm

elbow

armpit

lungs

skin

heart

heartbeat

arteries

veins

digestion

liver

stomach

touch

pump

intestines

bladder

adults

child

27

Materials

The world is made of many different materials. Some are rare, and some you might see every single day!

iron

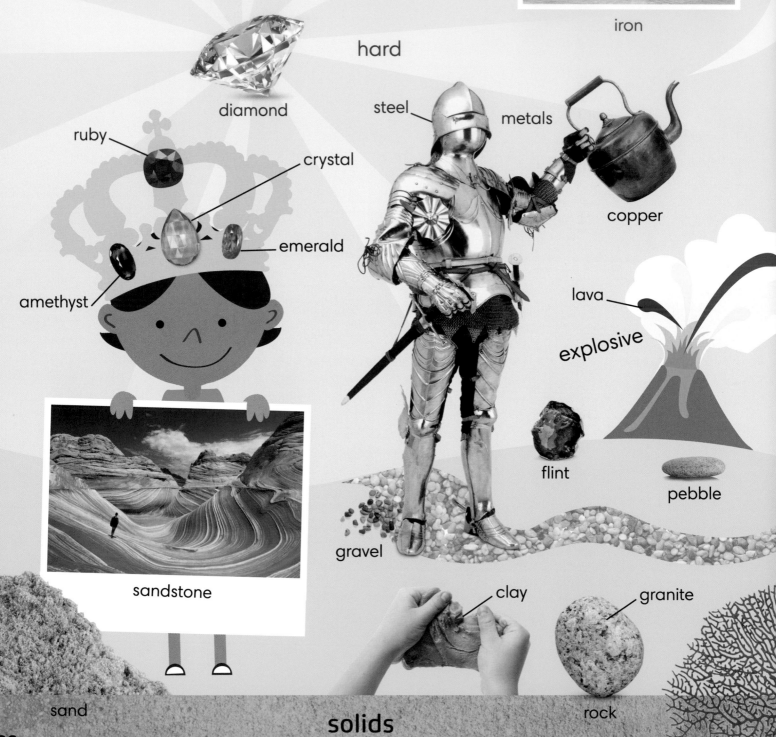

hard

diamond

ruby

crystal

emerald

amethyst

steel

metals

copper

lava

explosive

flint

pebble

sandstone

gravel

clay

granite

sand

solids

rock

ice crystal

icicle

freeze

melt

paper

oxygen

hydrogen

poisonous

nitrogen

carbon dioxide

salt crystal

sugar crystal

plastic

elastic

rubber band

air

man-made

gases

cotton

recyclable

biodegradable

wool

rain

natural

glass

water

wood

pearl

shell

acid

brittle

sponge

absorbent

washing-up liquid

coral

liquids

Underground

You can't always see it, but there is a whole world in the ground underneath your feet!

anthill

ants

microorganism

bulbs

insect

seeds

soil

roots

worm

clay

gerbil

badger

den

mole

fox

hamster

sett

jewellery

coins

warren

treasure

pot

rabbit

diamond

gold

tin

ruins

coal

fossil dinosaur skull

core

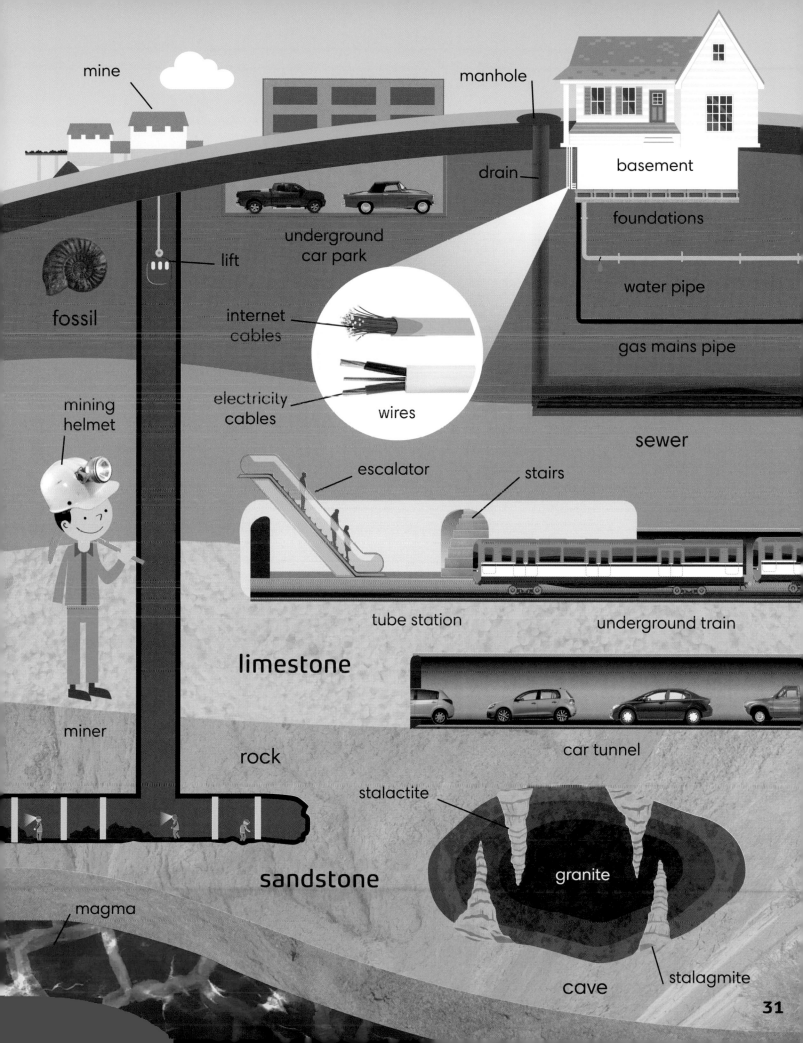

mine

manhole

basement

drain

foundations

fossil

lift

underground
car park

internet
cables

water pipe

gas mains pipe

electricity
cables

wires

sewer

mining
helmet

escalator

stairs

tube station

underground train

limestone

miner

rock

car tunnel

stalactite

sandstone

granite

magma

cave

stalagmite

Comparisons

You might be tall. You might be short. You might be early or late, or hot or cold. These kinds of words help us to describe and compare things.

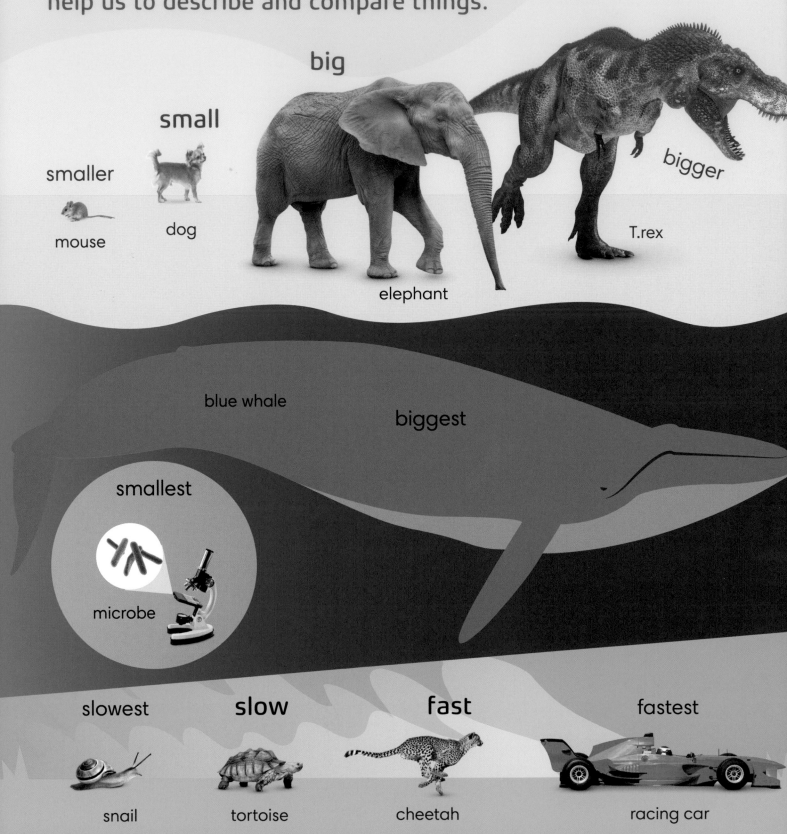

big

small

smaller

mouse

dog

elephant

bigger

T.rex

blue whale

biggest

smallest

microbe

slowest

slow

fast

fastest

snail

tortoise

cheetah

racing car

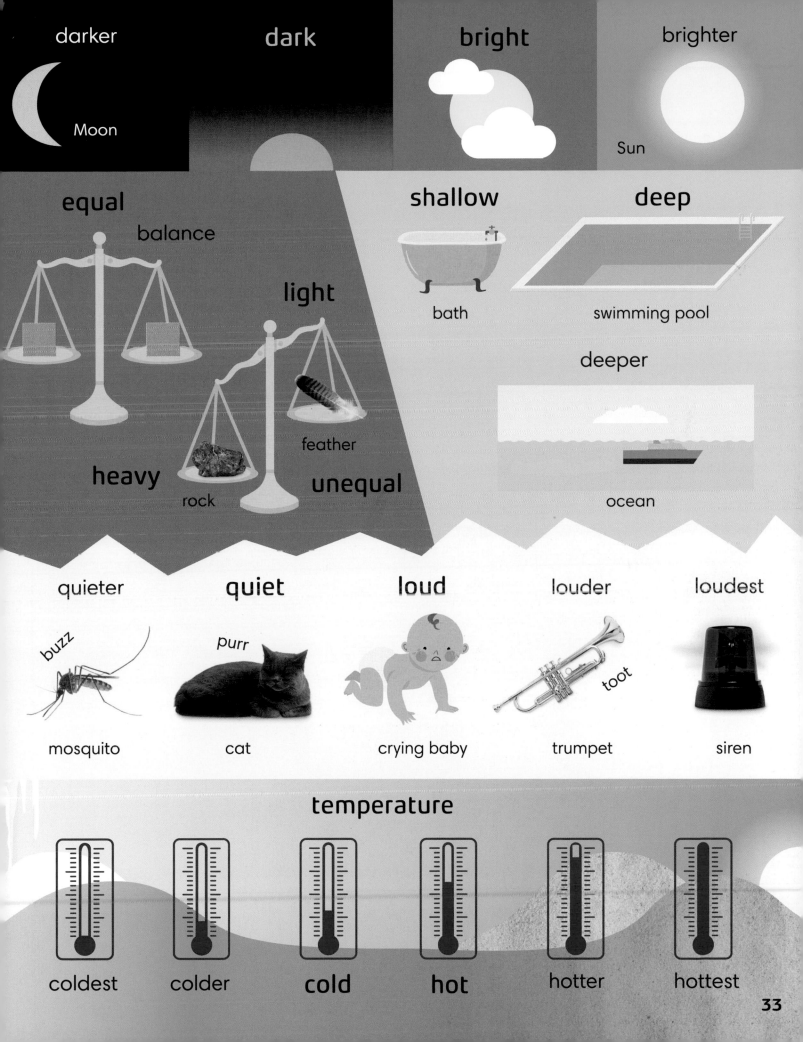

darker

Moon

dark

bright

brighter

Sun

equal

balance

light

heavy

rock

feather

unequal

shallow

bath

deep

swimming pool

deeper

ocean

quieter

buzz

mosquito

quiet

purr

cat

loud

crying baby

louder

toot

trumpet

loudest

siren

temperature

coldest

colder

cold

hot

hotter

hottest

33

Junk

What happens to all the things we throw away? How many of these things can be reused or recycled?

backhoe loader

electromagnet

steel

excavator

aluminium

landfill

repair

engine

reuse

windows

exhaust pipes

rubbish truck

dustbin

scrap

metal

junk

rubbish collector

rubber

tyres

crate

scrapyard

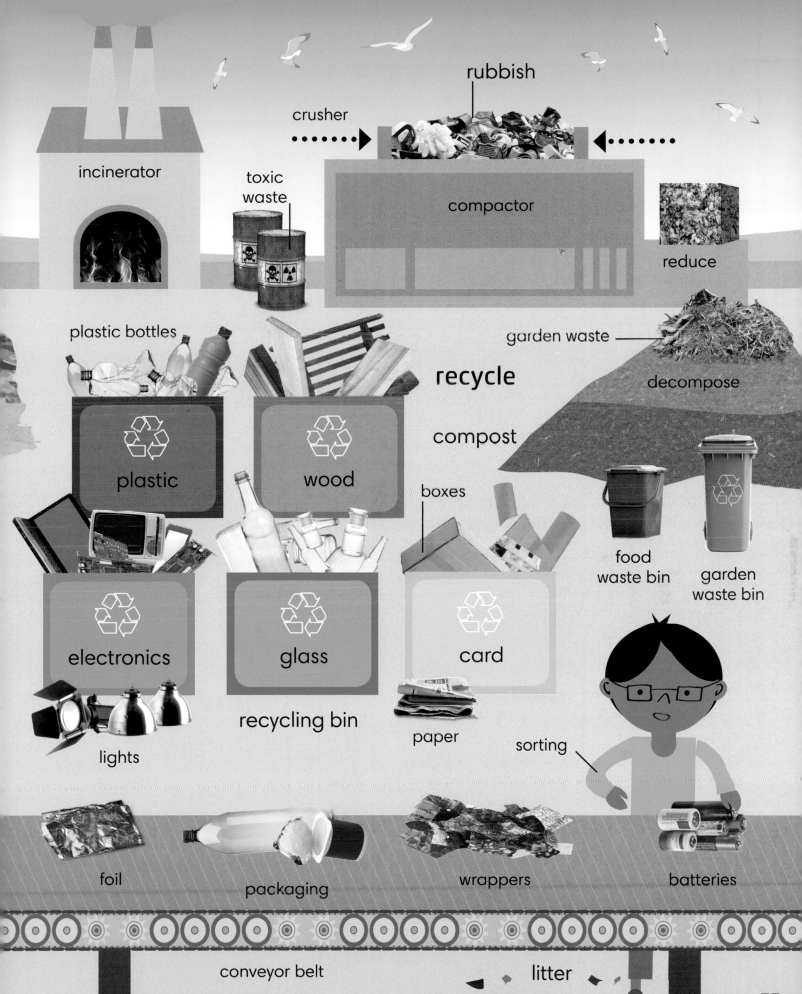

rubbish

crusher

incinerator

toxic waste

compactor

reduce

plastic bottles

garden waste

recycle

decompose

plastic

wood

compost

boxes

food waste bin

garden waste bin

electronics

glass

card

lights

recycling bin

paper

sorting

foil

packaging

wrappers

batteries

conveyor belt

litter

35

Measuring

If you are doing an experiment or making something, you often need to measure things. And there are many ways to measure things!

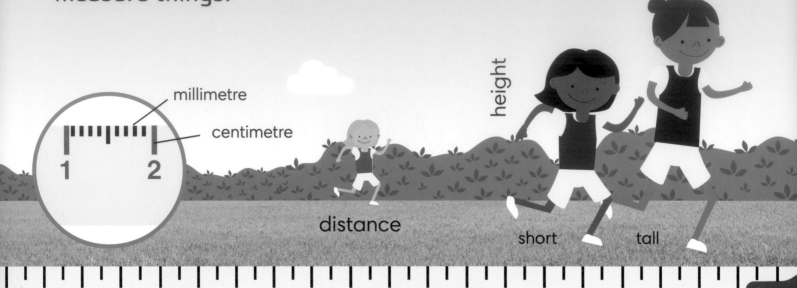

millimetre
centimetre

1   2

height

short   tall

distance

measuring tape

length

100 cm = 1 metre

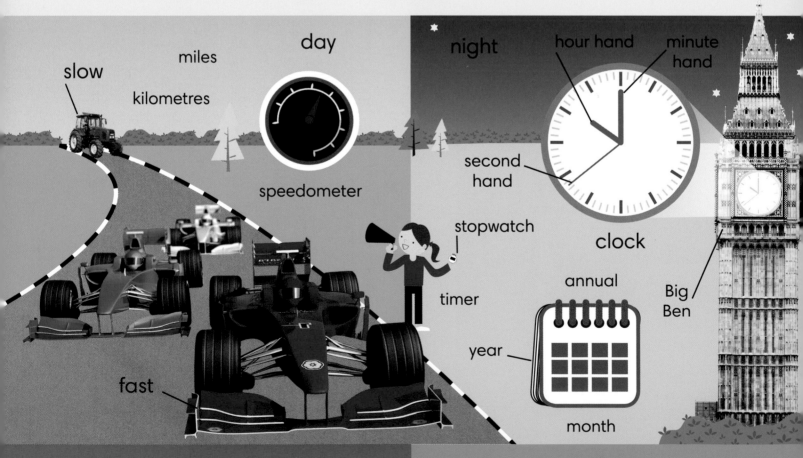

slow

miles

kilometres

day

speedometer

fast

timer

stopwatch

night

hour hand

minute hand

second hand

clock

Big Ben

annual

year

month

speed

time

money

99p

£2.00

notes

coins

light

shopping

heavy

weight

balance

gram

weighing scales

kilogram

apples

weight

hot

cold

thermometer

200⁰

degrees

temperature

fill

full

litre

half empty

half full

millilitres

container

volume

37

Up high

Look up! There are lots of things going on up there. What can you see above you?

ozone layer

atmosphere

clouds

cirrus clouds

stratus clouds

jet

Empire State Building

skyscrapers

gnat

helicopter

hot-air balloon

Eiffel Tower

thunder

lightning

The Shard

satellite dish

lightning rod

aerial

flag

helium balloons

kite

tower block

satellite

star

meteor

planet

Moon

Sun

jet stream

biplane

aeroplane

travel

hang glider

cumulus clouds

skydiver

glide

snowflakes

parachute

Chinook

pollen

rain

vapour trail

flying

red kite

seagull

birds

butterfly

pigeon

swallow

mountain

Everest

control tower

mist

wind turbine

windsock

phone mast

jet pack

39

Long ago

65 million years ago, dinosaurs were alive. 2.6 million years ago, large areas of the Earth were covered in ice. The Earth looks very different today.

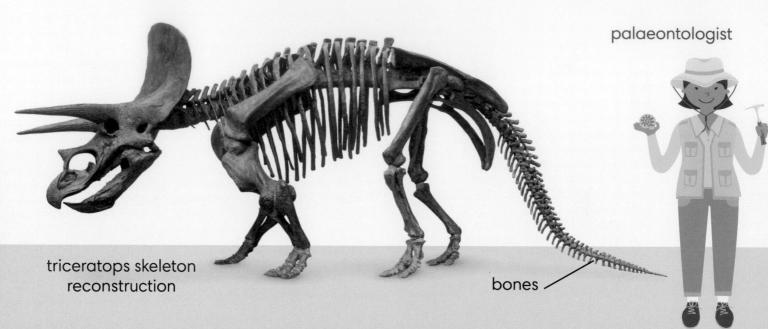

palaeontologist

triceratops skeleton
reconstruction

bones

fossils

albertosaurus skull

teeth

dinosaur poo

ammonite

amber

plesiosaur
foot

ichthyosaur

plesiosaur

horseshoe crab

meteor strike

microraptor

volcano

pine trees

diplodocus

dinosaurs

tyrannosaurus

triceratops

horsetail

dinosaur eggs

stegosaurus

ice age

saber tooth tiger

mammoth

giant ground sloth

Plants

Plants are really important to our planet. They make their food from the carbon dioxide we breathe out, and they release oxygen back into the air for us to breathe in.

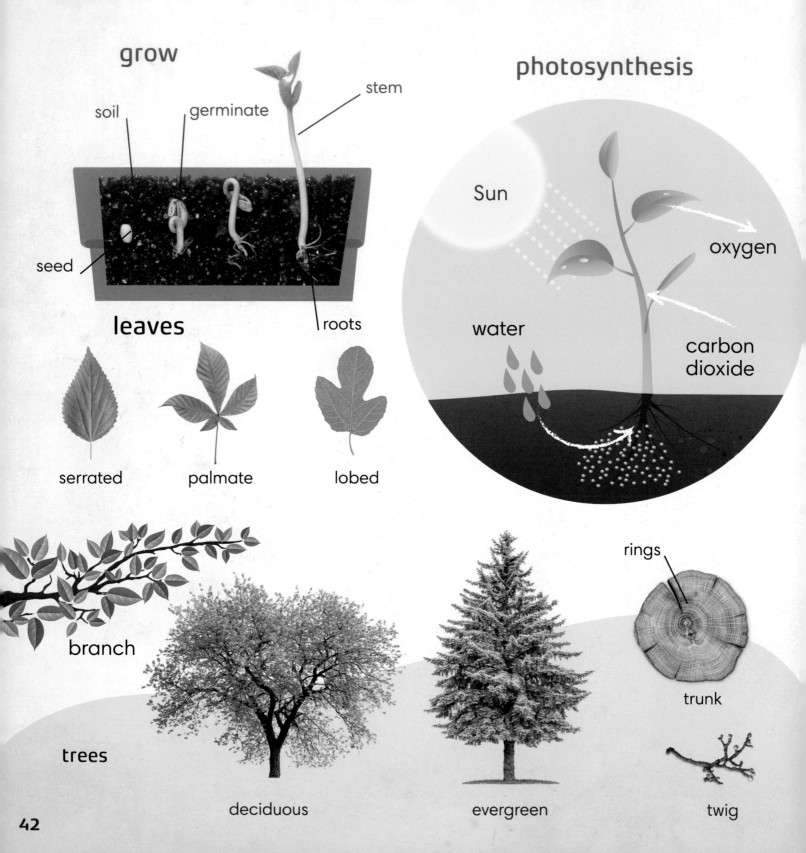

grow

soil

germinate

stem

seed

roots

photosynthesis

Sun

oxygen

water

carbon dioxide

leaves

serrated

palmate

lobed

branch

rings

trunk

trees

twig

deciduous

evergreen

flowers

stigma

stamen

bee

pollinator

ovary

pollen

butterfly

bud

blossom

petal

plants

green

pod

pine cone

soya beans

moss

climbing plant

cactus

fruits

stone

nuts

apple

avocado

mango

cherries

vegetables

radish

onion

asparagus

sweet potato

bulb

rhizome

root vegetable

tuber

43

Playground forces

It's fun to play at the park, but did you know that parks are full of science? You are using forces all the time when you play!

pull

push

friction

swing

force of gravity

force of gravity

slide

balance

push up

seesaw

force of gravity

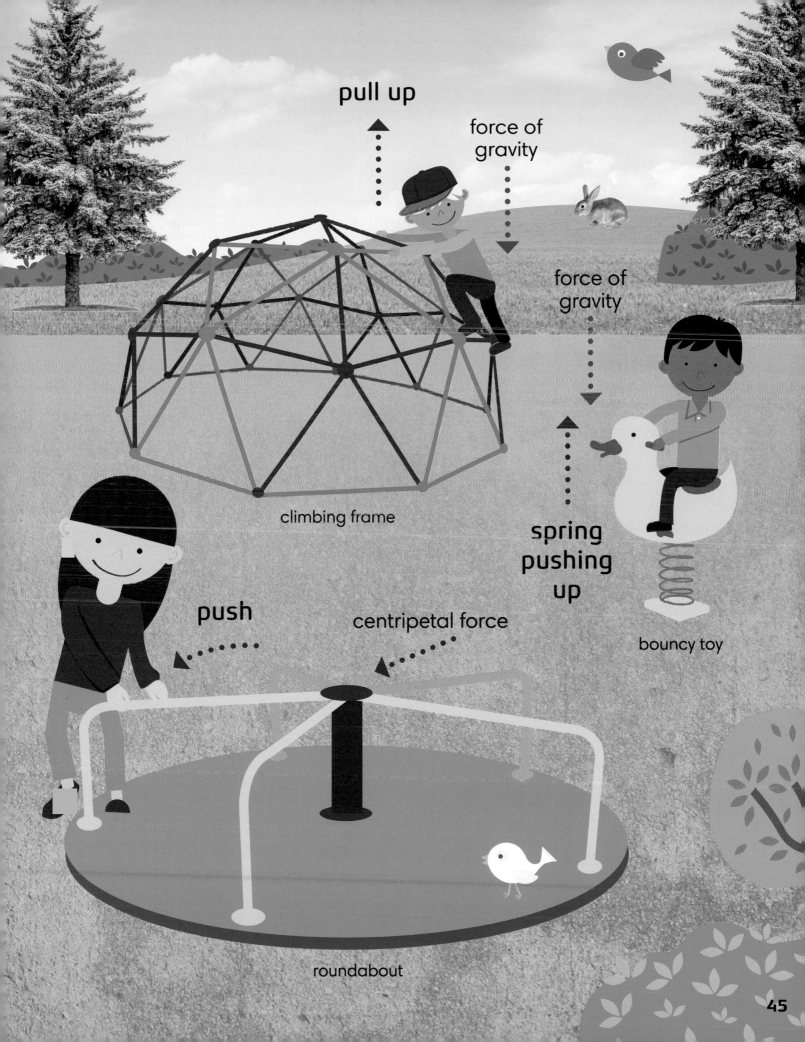

pull up

force of gravity

force of gravity

climbing frame

push

centripetal force

spring pushing up

bouncy toy

roundabout

45

Laboratory

Some scientists work in a laboratory. Different scientists use different equipment. What kind of scientist would you like to be?

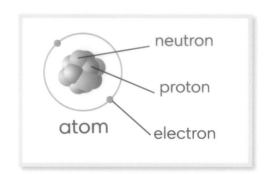

neutron

proton

atom

electron

evolution

chemistry

chemist

safety goggles

chemical

test tube

liquid

funnel

experiment

gas

mix

Bunsen burner

idea

conical flask

biologist

magnifying glass

observe

lab coat

biology

plant

H₂SO₄ KO

acid

zoologist

measure

animal

specimen jar

engineer

diagram

machine

laser

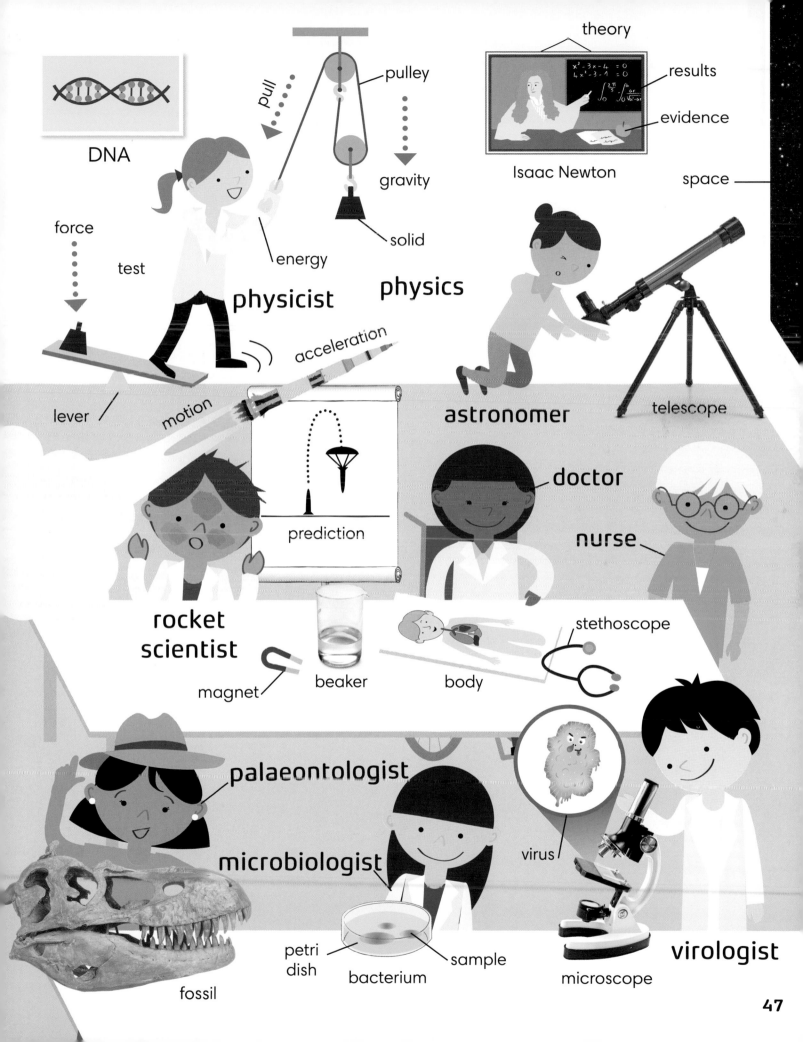

DNA

pull

pulley

gravity

solid

energy

force

test

physicist

physics

acceleration

lever

motion

theory

results

evidence

Isaac Newton

space

astronomer

telescope

doctor

nurse

prediction

rocket
scientist

stethoscope

magnet

beaker

body

palaeontologist

virus

microbiologist

petri
dish

sample

bacterium

virologist

microscope

fossil

Ecosystems

An ecosystem is a group of animals and plants living in a habitat, with different relationships to each other. Let's take a dip into the pond ecosystem. The arrows show how energy flows, and who benefits from each relationship.

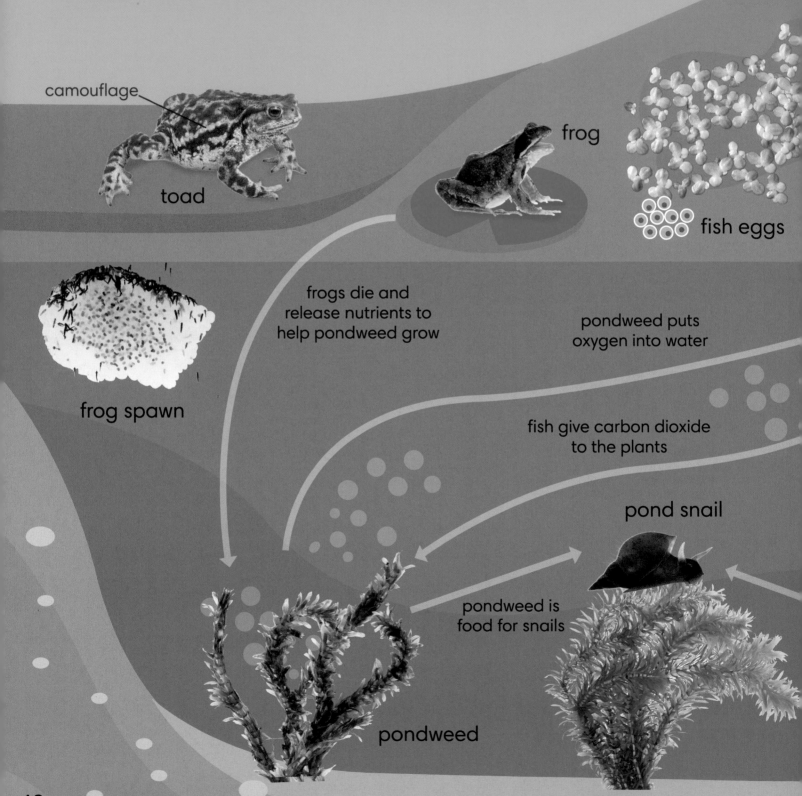

camouflage

toad

frog

fish eggs

frogs die and release nutrients to help pondweed grow

pondweed puts oxygen into water

frog spawn

fish give carbon dioxide to the plants

pond snail

pondweed is food for snails

pondweed

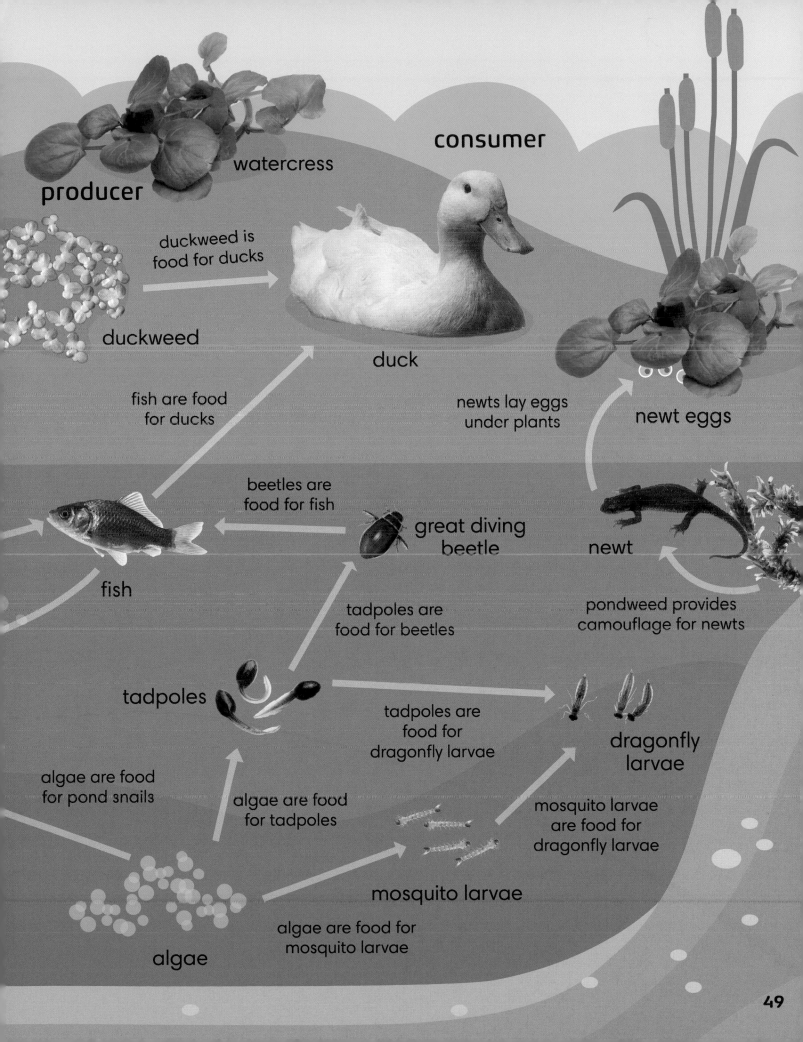

producer

watercress

consumer

duckweed is
food for ducks

duckweed

duck

fish are food
for ducks

newts lay eggs
under plants

newt eggs

beetles are
food for fish

great diving
beetle

newt

fish

tadpoles are
food for beetles

pondweed provides
camouflage for newts

tadpoles

tadpoles are
food for
dragonfly larvae

dragonfly
larvae

algae are food
for pond snails

algae are food
for tadpoles

mosquito larvae
are food for
dragonfly larvae

mosquito larvae

algae are food for
mosquito larvae

algae

Classification of animals

Animals are classified, or grouped together, with others that have the same features. Look at all the different kinds of animal there are.

jellyfish

coelenterates

myriapods

millipede

centipede

worms

roundworm

flatworm

echinoderms

starfish

sea urchin

molluscs

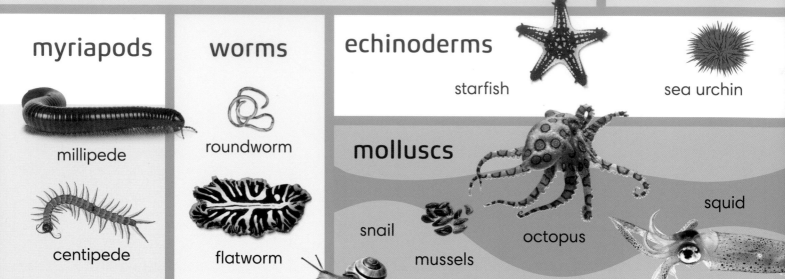

snail

mussels

octopus

squid

crustaceans

lobster

sea monkey

crab

shrimp

arachnids

spider

insects

beetle

fly

bee

butterfly

stick insect

scorpion

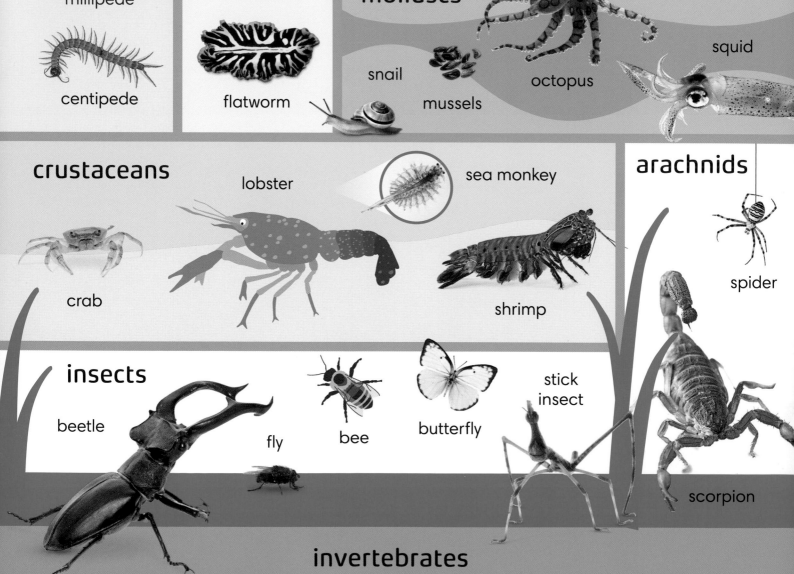

invertebrates

birds

owl

penguin

duck

chicken

mammals

horse

human

polar bear

dog

rabbit

marsupials

duck-billed platypus

koala

cat

kangaroo

lion

elephant

amphibians

newt

frog

toad

reptiles

snake

tortoise

crocodile

fish

clownfish

ray

shark

tuna

vertebrates

Water

Water comes from many sources, including a tap! There is so much of it on Earth that our planet looks blue from space.

ocean

blue planet

aqueduct

lake

freshwater

reservoir

ice cubes

drink

H₂O (water)

flood

stream

river

waterwheel

well

canal

irrigation

dam

shadoof

surf

riptide

wave

current

reef

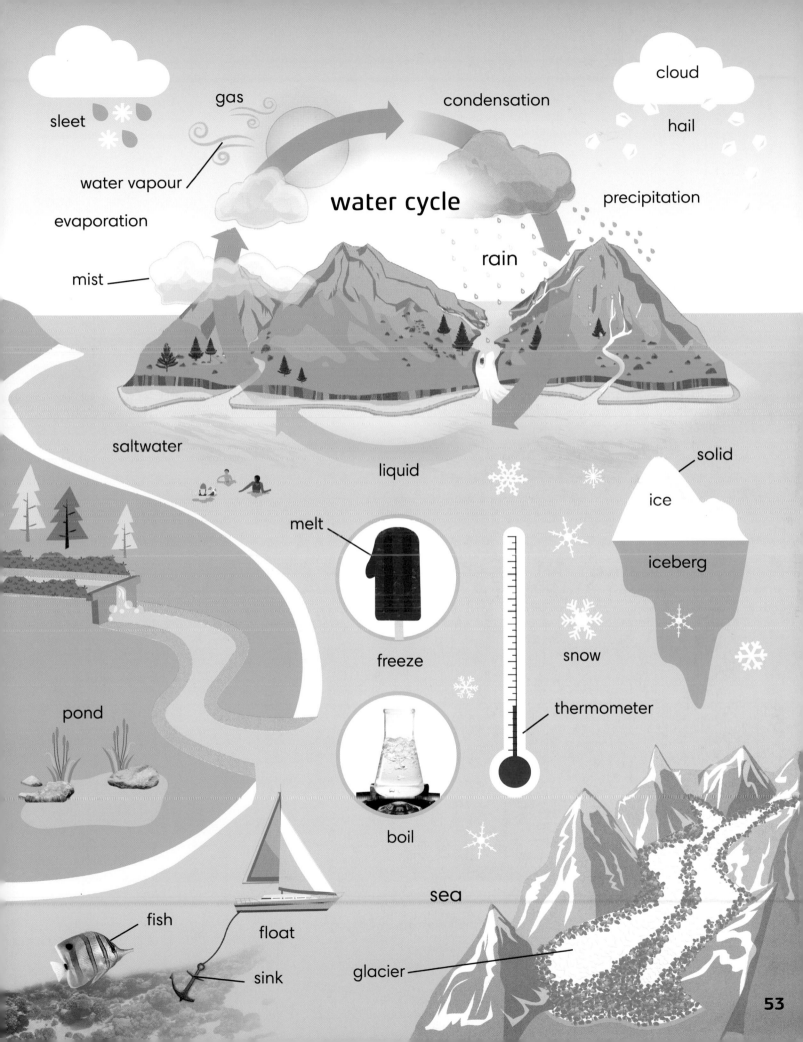

sleet

gas

condensation

cloud

hail

water vapour

evaporation

water cycle

precipitation

mist

rain

saltwater

solid

liquid

ice

melt

iceberg

freeze

snow

thermometer

pond

boil

sea

fish

float

glacier

sink

53

Experiments

Have you ever wanted to carry out an experiment?
Here are some things you might need.

equipment

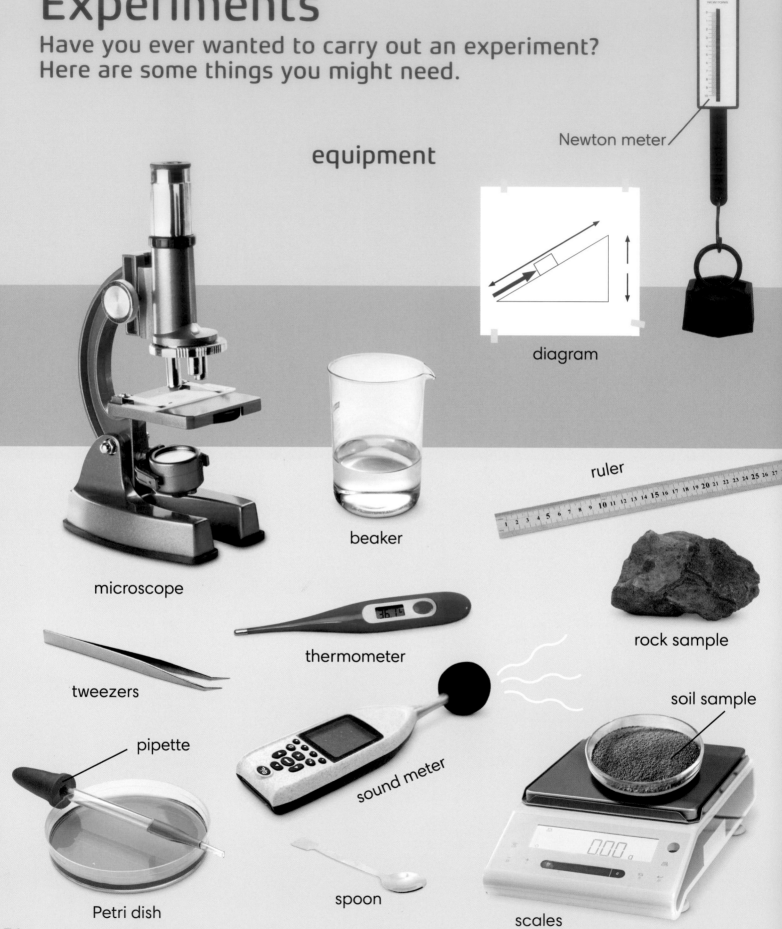

Newton meter

diagram

microscope

beaker

ruler

rock sample

tweezers

thermometer

pipette

sound meter

soil sample

Petri dish

spoon

scales

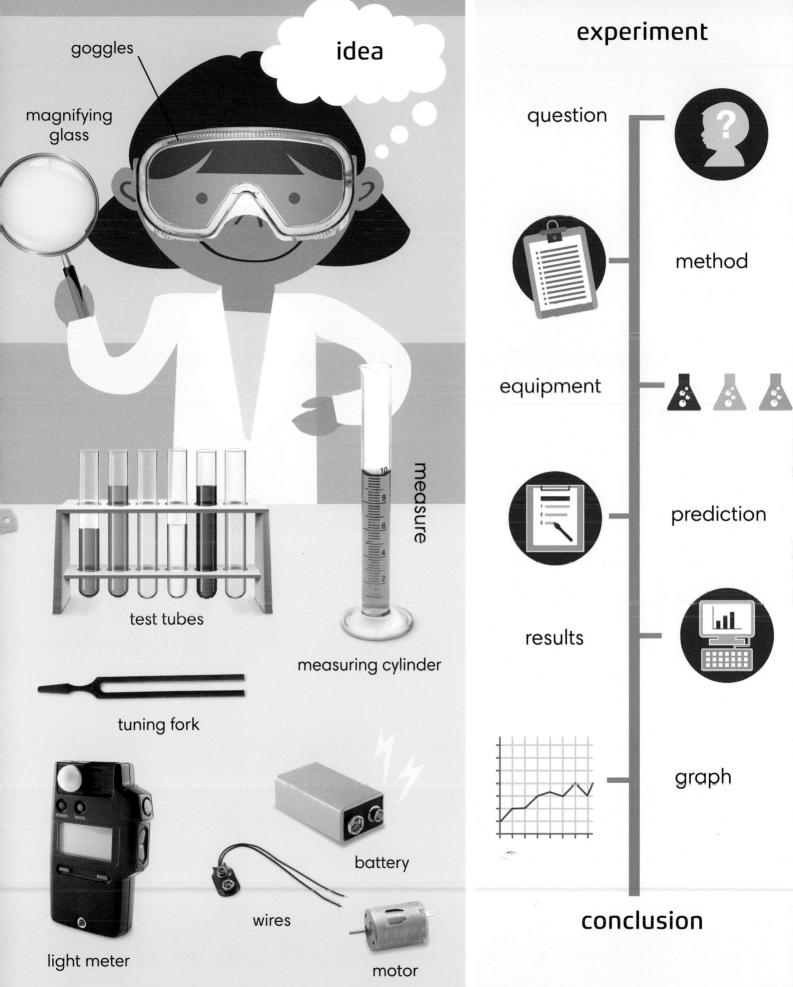

idea

goggles

magnifying glass

test tubes

measuring cylinder

measure

tuning fork

light meter

wires

battery

motor

experiment

question

method

equipment

prediction

results

graph

conclusion

55

Mixing and cooking

When you mix ingredients together, or heat them or cool them, you might end up making something new.

microwave

mixer

solid

weighing scales

blender

mould

preserve

pickle

oven

roast

burn

cook

steam

bubble

mould

thermometer

simmer

raw

hob

boil

timer

coffee
maker

wood-fired oven

fridge

freezer

bake

smoke

barbeque

sieve

whisk

charcoal

fire

heat

mix

combine

prove

campfire

57

Light

We need light in order to see. Light comes from a variety of sources. The source of light we use most is the Sun.

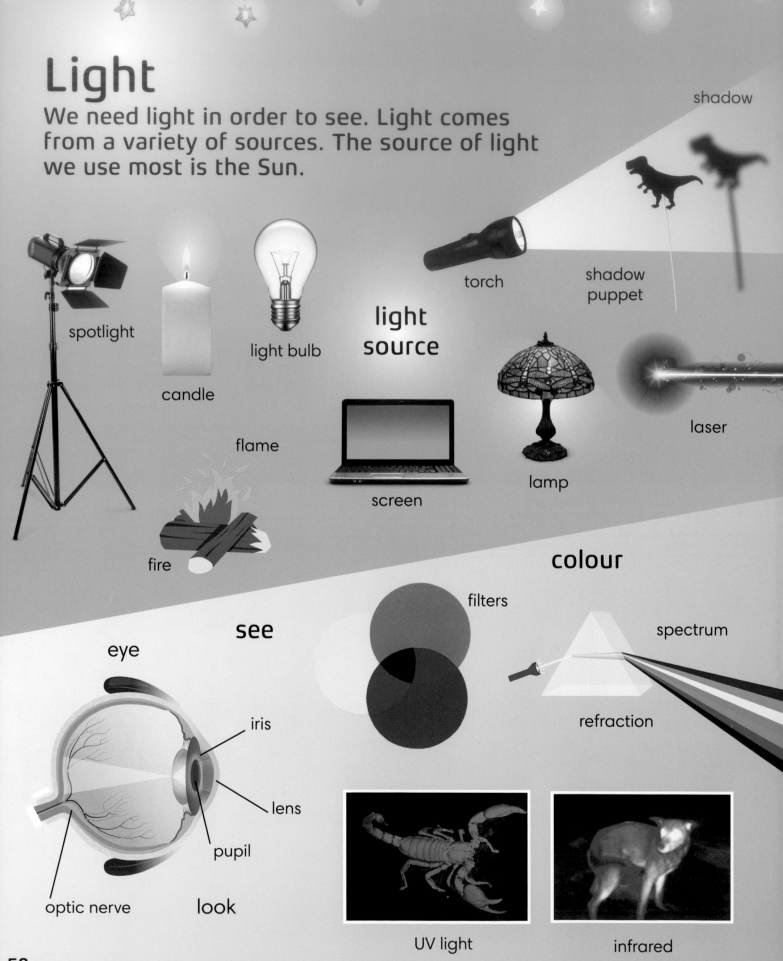

shadow

spotlight

candle

flame

fire

light bulb

light source

screen

torch

shadow puppet

lamp

laser

colour

see

eye

iris

lens

pupil

optic nerve

look

filters

refraction

spectrum

UV light

infrared

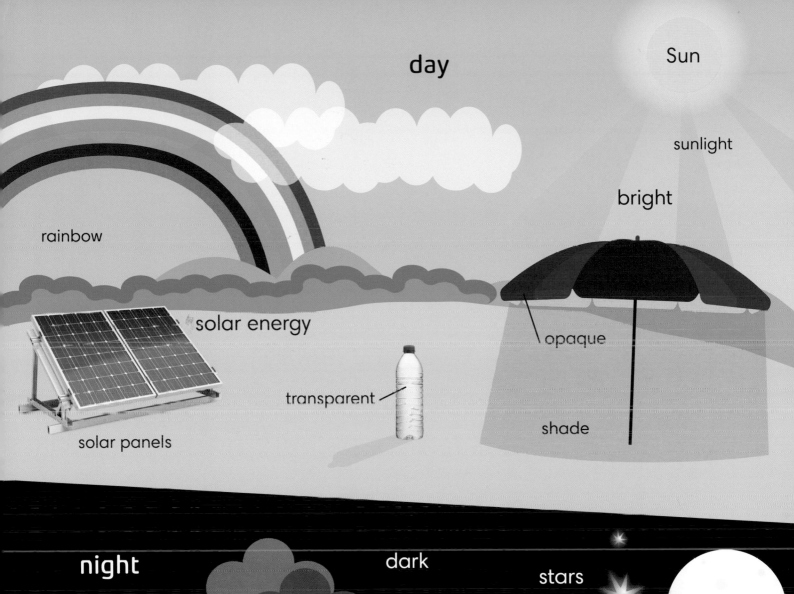

day

Sun

sunlight

bright

rainbow

solar energy

opaque

transparent

shade

solar panels

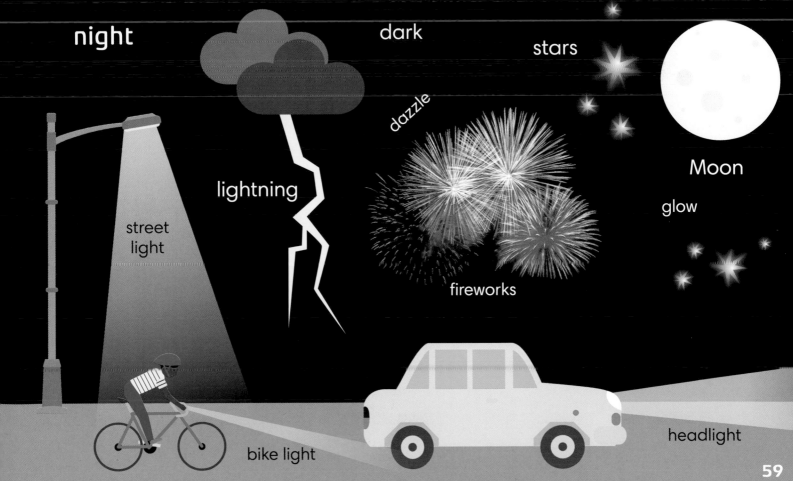

night

dark

stars

dazzle

Moon

lightning

glow

street
light

fireworks

bike light

headlight

Sharing and grouping

Some things come in pairs or in larger groups. We may need to share them out – one for me and one for you!

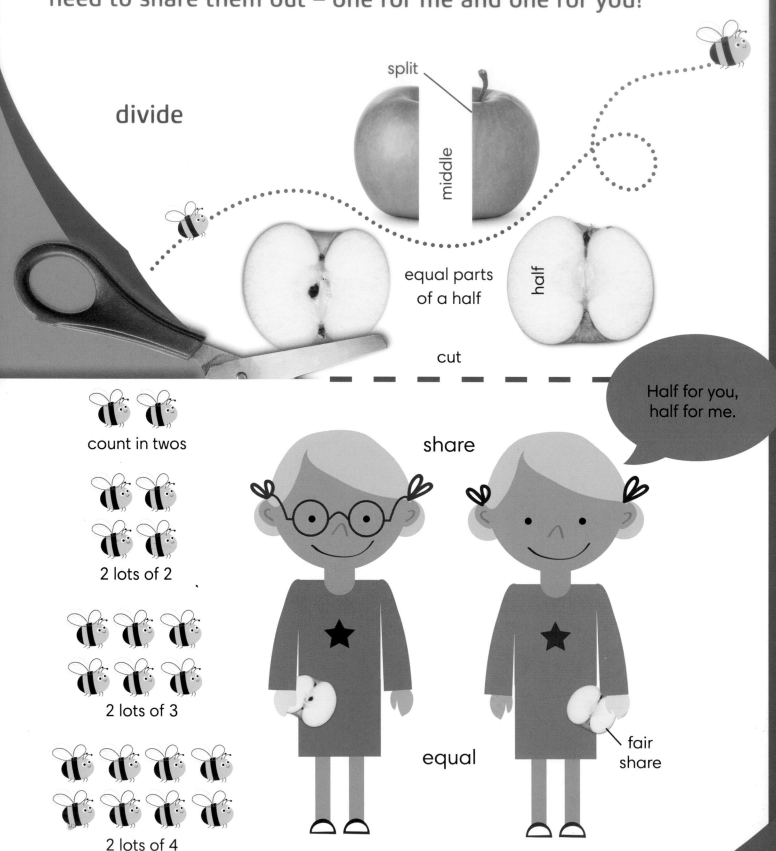

divide

split

middle

equal parts of a half

half

cut

count in twos

2 lots of 2

2 lots of 3

2 lots of 4

share

Half for you, half for me.

equal

fair share

60

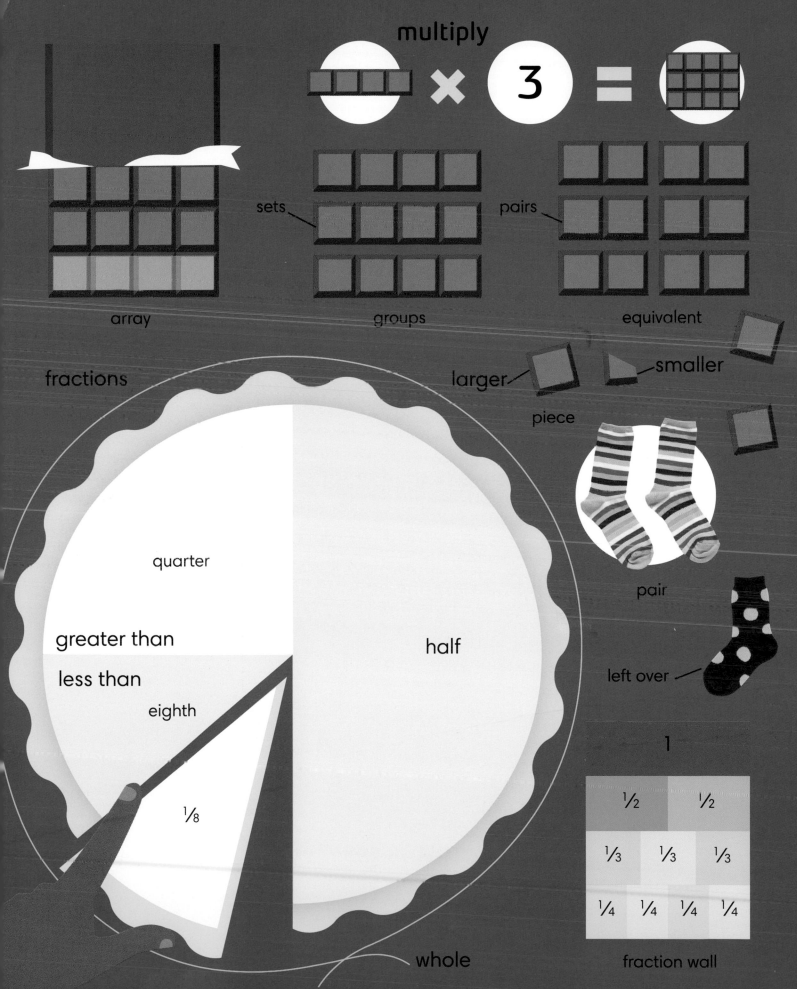

multiply

$\times$ 3 =

array

sets

groups

pairs

equivalent

fractions

larger

smaller

piece

pair

left over

quarter

greater than

less than

eighth

half

¹⁄₈

1

whole

½		½
⅓	⅓	⅓
¼	¼	¼	¼

fraction wall

Adding and subtracting

How many do you have? Have some been added or taken away? We need different words to describe how the number of things change.

sum

plus

all together   total

pairs that make 10

1	2	3	4	5	6	7	8	9	10
11	12	13	14	15	16	17	18	19	20
21	22	23	24	25	26	27	28	29	30
31	32	33	34	35	36	37	38	39	40
41	42	43	44	45	46	47	48	49	50
51	52	53	54	55	56	57	58	49	60
61	62	63	64	65	66	67	68	69	70
71	72	73	74	75	76	77	78	79	80
81	82	83	84	85	86	87	88	89	90
91	92	93	94	95	96	97	98	99	100

100 square

combine

one more

more

another one

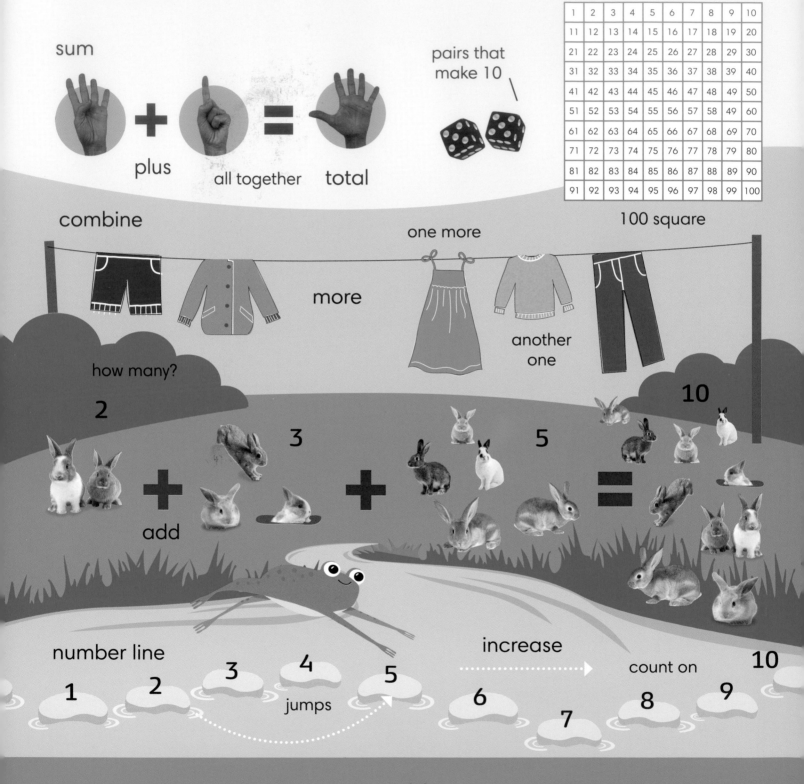

how many?

2

3

5

10

add

number line   increase   count on   10

1   2   3   4   5   jumps   6   7   8   9

add

partition

12 = 10 + 2

fewer

many

minus

2

1

1

less

what is left?

one less

how many?

blast off!

decrease

count back

number

0   1   2   3   4   5   6   7   8   9   10

subtract

Acknowledgments

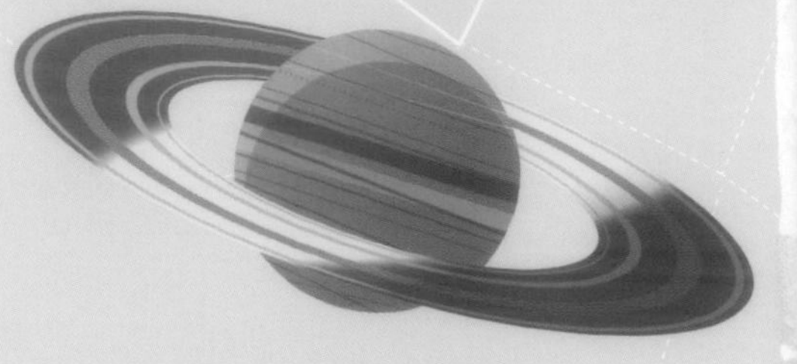

The publisher would like to thank the following for their kind permission to reproduce their photographs:

(Key: a-above; b-below/bottom; c-centre; f-far; l-left; r-right; t-top)

1 123RF.com: Kittipong Jirasukhanont (tc); likelike (br). Depositphotos Inc: joachimopelka (fbr). Dorling Kindersley: Natural History Museum, London (crb/Skull); Senckenberg Gesellshaft Fuer Naturforschugn Museum (bl). Dreamstime.com: Aomvector (clb); Icefront (tl); Macrovector (cb); Krungchingpixs (crb). 2 123RF.com: Fernando Gregory Milan (tr). Getty Images: Science Photo Library / Sergii Iaremenko (tl). 3 123RF.com: phive2015 (clb). 6-7 Dreamstime.com: Hospitalera; Orlando Florin Rosu (b). 6 Alamy Stock Photo: D. Hurst (bc). Dorling Kindersley: Liberty's Owl, Raptor and Reptile Centre, Hampshire, UK (cb). Dreamstime.com: Stan Ioan-alin / Stanalin (cl); Joystockphoto (tr). Getty Images / iStock: Sieboldianus (clb). 7 123RF.com: Eric Isselee (bc). Dreamstime.com: Aomvector (cra); Joystockphoto (t); Photodeti (tl); Dirk Ercken / Kikkerdirk (tc); Iakov Filimonov / jackf (c); Miramisska (crb); Onyxprj (br). 8 Dorling Kindersley: Peter Anderson (crb). Dreamstime.com: Iakov Filimonov / Jackf (ca); Kellyrichardsonfl (bl); Hospitalera (clb). Getty Images / iStock: RinoCdZ (c). 9 123RF.com: Eric Isselee / isselee (cr); Eric Isselee (cr/sheep); Anatolii Tsekhmister / tsekhmister (cb/rabbit). Dorling Kindersley: Peter Anderson (cl). Dreamstime.com: Ziga Camernik (bl); Stephanie Frey (ca/nest); Josef Skacel (tr); Anton Ignatenco (cra); Damian Palus (cla); Rudmer Zwerver / Creativenature1 (bc). Fotolia: Csaba Vanyi / emprise (cb). Getty Images / iStock: RinoCdZ (ca). 10 Dreamstime.com: Alexxl66 (cb); Dreamzdesigner (ca); Nexus7 (tr). 11 123RF.com: 29mokara (cb); Aleksandr Ermolaev (cl); Brian Kinney (crb/aeroplane). Dorling Kindersley: Aberdeen Fire Department, Maryland (clb); Bate Collection (cla). Dreamstime.com: Jiri Hera (cra); Nerthuz (tr); Isselee (c); Michael Truchon / Mtruchon (crb). 12 123RF.com: Milic Djurovic (cla); Valery Voennyy / vvoennyy (cb). Dreamstime.com: Nerthuz (tr); Radub85 (ftr). 13 123RF.com: Micha? Giel / gielmichal (tr); manaemedia (tc); Richard Thomas (crb); nerthuz (bl). Dorling Kindersley: James Mann / David Riman (br); Toro Wheelhorse UK Ltd (c); National Railway Museum, New Dehli (bc). Dreamstime.com: Carlos Caetano (ca); Andrey Navrotskiy (cla); Andres Rodriguez / Andresr (cra); Tuulijumala (cra/phone); Shariff Che' Lah / Shariffc (cb). 14 123RF.com: Kittipong Jirasukhanont (bc); mopic (c). Dreamstime.com: Torian Dixon / Mrincredible (cb); Levgenii Tryfonov / Trifff (bl). 15 123RF.com: solarseven (c). Alamy Stock Photo: Jupiterimages (clb). Dorling Kindersley: Andy Crawford (tl). Dreamstime.com: Viktarm (crb). ESO: (br). Getty Images: Steffen Schnur (cra). Unsplash: Jongsun Lee / @sarahleejs (tr). 16 Alamy Stock Photo: NASA Photo (clb). Dorling Kindersley: Science Museum, London (br/x2). Dreamstime.com: Titoonz (bl). NASA: (cla, cra, crb). 16-17 Dreamstime.com: Astrofireball (b); Nerthuz (ca). 17 Dorling Kindersley: Andy Crawford / Bob Gathany (ca); Science Museum, London (bl/x2); NASA (cr). Dreamstime.com: Igor Korionov (br); Philcold (tr). NASA: (clb); NASA Goddard / Arizona State University (bc). 18 123RF.com: nerthuz (crb). Dorling Kindersley: National Motor Museum Beaulieu (cla); Skoda UK (c). Dreamstime.com: Leonello Calvetti (b); Mlan61 (cra); Haiyin (cl); Michal Zacharzewski / Mzacha (cr); Vincentstthomas (cb). 19 Dorling Kindersley: Llandrindod Wells National Cycle Museum Wales (br); J.D Tandems (crb). Dreamstime.com: Bob Phillips / Digital69 (tc); Marinko Tarlac / Mangia (tl); Tacettin Ulas / Photofactoryulas (tr); Olga Samorodova (ca); Vladvitek (cb). 20 Dorling Kindersley: Fleet Air Arm Museum (cla); Tanks, Trucks and Firepower Show (c); The Tank Museum, Bovington (cr); James River Equipment (br). Dreamstime.com: Eugene Berman (tr); Mlan61 (clb); Photobac (crb). 21 123RF.com: Robert Churchill (cb). Dorling Kindersley: Doubleday Swineshead (tr); George Manning (cr); Matthew Ward (tc/Land Rover). Dreamstime.com: Nikolay Antonov (tl); Natursports (cl); Robwilson39 (crb); Classic Vector (cra); Shariff Che' Lah / Shariffc (cra/Car); Soleg1974 (cla); Topgeek (ca); Gradts (tc); Eric Isselée / Isselee (tc/Horse). Getty Images / iStock: DigitalVision Vectors / filo (bl); dumayne (bc). 22 123RF.com: alhovik (br); Andrey Armyagov / cookelma (b); Serg_v (t). Dreamstime.com: Marilyn Gould / Marilyngould (clb). 23 Dreamstime.com: Rita Jayaraman / Margorita (cb); Mike Ricci (tr); Zuberka (clb). Getty Images / iStock: E+ / miljko (cra); mysticenergy (t). 24 Dreamstime.com: Radub85 (cla). 25 123RF.com: jovannig (c). Dreamstime.com: Tartilastock (br, ca). Getty Images / iStock: DigitalVision Vectors / diane555 (clb). 26 Dreamstime.com: Radub85 (bl). 27 123RF.com: tribalium123 (cb). Alamy Stock Photo: Design Pics Inc. (clb). Dreamstime.com: Anton Ignatenco (cr). 28 123RF.com: Maria Wachala (tr). Dorling Kindersley: Alan Keohane (cra); Natural History Museum, London (cl). Dreamstime.com: Photka (bl). Fotolia: apttone (ca). Getty Images / iStock: wanderluster (clb). 28-29 Dreamstime.com: Charlotte Lake (b). 29 Dreamstime.com: BY (ca); Coolmintproductions (tl); Ruslan Gilmanshin (clb); Dmstudio (cb); Jianghongyan (clb/log); Valentyn75 (cb/oyster); Puripat Khummungkhoon (crb). 30 Dorling Kindersley: Durham University Oriental Museum (cb); Natural History Museum, London (bc); Holts Gems (crb). Dreamstime.com: Richard Griffin (cra); Isselee (cl); Irina Tischenko / Irochka (ca). Fotolia: apttone (cb/diamond). Getty Images / iStock: UrosPoteko (cla). 30-31 Dreamstime.com: Mansum008 (bc). Getty Images: Ratnakorn Piyasirisorost. 31 123RF.com: klotz (cl). Dorling Kindersley: Skoda UK (ca). Dreamstime.com: Georgii Dolgykh / Gdolgikh (cb); Maksim Toome / Mtoome (crb); Whilerests (crb/coupe car); Konstantinos Moraitis (fcrb). 32 123RF.com: leonello calvetti (cra); Andrzej Tokarski / ajt (bl). Dreamstime.com: Andrey Burmakin (ca); Elena Schweitzer / Egal (clb/Microscope); Andrey Sukhachev / Nchuprin (clb); Isselee (bc); Stu Porter / Stuporter (bc/Cheetah); Shariff Che' Lah / Shariffc (br). 33 123RF.com: bovalentino (crb/Siren). Dorling Kindersley: Natural History Museum, London (ca). Dreamstime.com: Johannesk (cl); Yifang Zhao (crb); Ihor Smishko (br). 34 123RF.com: Roman Samokhin (cra). Dreamstime.com: Buriy (bl/Scrap); Nagy-bagoly Ilona (bl); Sarawuth Pamoon (bl/Pipe); Dan Van Den Broeke / Dvande (cra/Electromagnet, cla); Photobac (ca); Dmitry Rukhlenko (crb/x 2). 35 123RF.com: serezniy (fclb/Light); Tomasz Trybus / irontrybex (fcla); Anton Starikov (cl). Dorling Kindersley: Quinn Glass, Britvic, Fentimans (clb, cb/Bottle); Science Museum, London (fclb); Jemma Westing / Dave King (cb). Dreamstime.com: Péter Gudella (fcl); Stephen Sweet / Cornishman (cla); Maglara (cla/Table); Robert Wisdom (fcl/Laptop); Vladimir Ovchinnikov / Djahan (fclb/Tablet); Yury Shirokov / Yuris (crb); Rangizzz (cr). Getty Images / iStock: CasarsaGuru (cra); worradirek (tc); Picsfive (fcla/Bottles); t_kimura (fcr). 36 123RF.com: Serg_v (ca). Dreamstime.com: Soleg1974 (clb). Getty Images / iStock: franckreporter (br); Henrik5000 (bl). 37 Dreamstime.com: Allexxandar (br); AWesleyFloyd (cra); Anton Ignatenco (cra/apples). Getty Images / iStock: TheArtist (tr). 38 Dorling Kindersley: Claire Cordier (bl); Royal International Air Tattoo 2011 (ca). Dreamstime.com: Icefront (cla); Kirati Kicharearn (cl); Snake3d (clb). 39 123RF.com: Kittipong Jirasukhanont (tl); solarseven (tc); pteshka (cla); Oksana Tkachuk (fcr). Dorling Kindersley: Chris Gomersall Photography (clb). Dreamstime.com: 3drenderings (bl); Bob Phillips / Digital69 (fcra); Torsakarin (cra); Steve Mann / The_guitar_mann (cra/Helicopter); Dmitry Pichugin / Dmitryp (b); Domiciano Pablo Romero Franco (cb). 40 123RF.com: alexeykonovalenko (clb). Dorling Kindersley: Natural History Museum, London (crb, crb/Plesiosaur); Senckenberg Gesellshaft Fuer Naturforschugn Museum (ca); Natural History Museum (br). Dreamstime.com: Mr1805 (bl, bc). 41 123RF.com: leonello calvetti (cra); virtexie (cl). Dorling Kindersley: Natural History Museum, London (cla). Dreamstime.com: Valentyna Chukhlyebova (crb); Digitalstormcinema (bl); Corey A Ford (bc). 42 123RF.com: likelike (cl). Depositphotos Inc: joachimopelka (c). Dreamstime.com: Alexey Borodin (crb); Krungchingpixs (fcl); Schondrienn (clb); Vaclav Volrab (bc); Zerbor (bc/Pine); Wawritto (cr). 42-43 Dreamstime.com: Designprintck. 43 123RF.com: Natthakan Jommanee (fclb); Oleg Palii (c). Dreamstime.com: Abrakadabraart (bl); Peterfactors (tc, cla); Anphotos (tr); Alfio Scisetti (cr); Oleksandr Panchenko (cl); Domnitsky (fcl); Anton Ignatenco (clb); Katerina Kovaleva (cb); HongChan001 (crb); Tihis (fcrb); Gongxin (br). 44 123RF.com: Richard E Leighton Jr (cb). Dreamstime.com: Svetlana Larina / Blair_witch (clb). 44-45 123RF.com: Serg_v (ca). Dreamstime.com: Charlotte Lake (b). 45 Dreamstime.com: Zerbor (tl, tr). 46 Dreamstime.com: Andrii Iarygin (cr); Smallow (crb); Hermin Utomo / Herminutomo (br). Fotolia: Auris (clb/x2). Getty Images: MirageC (cla). 47 Dorling Kindersley: Natural History Museum, London (bl). Dreamstime.com: Michał Rojek / Michalrojek (tr); trekandshoot (cra); Elena Schweitzer / Egal (br). 48 Alamy Stock Photo: Chris Mattison (cla). Dreamstime.com: Isselee (crb); Jgade (ca). 48-49 Dreamstime.com: Sensovision (ca/x2). 49 123RF.com: Pan Demin (crb). Dreamstime.com: Tatsuya Otsuka (tl, cra); Palex66 (cb). 50 123RF.com: Sommai Larkjit (clb); Pavlo Vakhrushev / vapi (tr). Dorling Kindersley: Linda Pitkin (c). Dreamstime.com: Cynoclub (bl); Isselee (crb); Domiciano Pablo Romero Franco (cb). 51 123RF.com: Yuliia Sonsedska (cr). Dorling Kindersley: Twan Leenders (clb). Dreamstime.com: Mikhail Blajenov / Starper (crb); Kotomiti_okuma (tl); Eric Isselée / Isselee (tc); Olha Lytvynenko (cla); Jgade (clb/Frog); Zweizug (br); Isselee (cra). Fotolia: Eric Isselee (cla/Koala). 52 Dorling Kindersley: NASA (tr). Dreamstime.com: Eyewave (cla); Paul Fleet / Paulfleet (c); Paul Topp / Nalukai (bl); Jesue92 (br). 52-53 123RF.com: mihtiander (bc). 53 Dorling Kindersley: Peter Anderson (clb). Getty Images / iStock: marrio31 (bl). 54 123RF.com: anmbph (cb/Thermometer). Dreamstime.com: Jörg Beuge (bl); Dmitriy Melnikov / Dgm007 (cla); Feng Yu (clb); Catalinr (bc); Puntasit Choksawatdikorn (cb); Raisa Muzipova (cra); Irina Brinza (cr); Fokinol (crb); Chernetskaya (crb/Soil); Kwanchaichaiudom (br). 55 Dreamstime.com: Szerdahelyi Adam (bl); Yael Weiss (fcla); Macrovector (cl); Mohammed Anwarul Kabir Choudhury (c); Nongpimmy (r/x5); Ylivdesign (cra). Getty Images: MirageC (cla). 56 123RF.com: bagwold (cra); Milosh Kojadinovich (ca/Jelly). Dreamstime.com: Cynoclub (c); Emin Ozkan (cla); Sergioua (ca); Nexus7 (cl); Drohn88 (cr); Olga Popova (clb); Witold Krasowski / Witoldkr1 (bl). 57 Dreamstime.com: Mihajlo Becej (cla); Anton Starikov (clb); Lukas Gojda (br); Makc76 (tr); Design56 (tl). 58 123RF.com: phive2015 (ca); serezniy (fcla). Dorling Kindersley: Stephen Oliver (cb). Dreamstime.com: Natalya Aksenova (cla); Augusto Cabral / Gubh83 (cra); Margojh (cr); Robert Wisdom (c); Carla F. Castagno / Korat_cn (br). Fotolia: Matthew Cole (ca/Torch). 59 Alamy Stock Photo: Jan Miks (cb). Dreamstime.com: BY (ca); Nikolay Plotnikov (bl). Getty Images / iStock: spawns (cla). 62 123RF.com: pixelrobot (ca); Тимур Конев (cla); Anatolii Tsekhmister / tsekhmister (cb, crb/Brown bunny). Dreamstime.com: Pavel Sazonov (cr, cb/White rabbit). Fotolia: Stefan Andronache (clb/2 Rabbits, crb/2 Rabbits). Getty Images: Mike Kemp (clb, crb/Jumping rabbit). 63 123RF.com: Maria Averburg (tr). Dreamstime.com: Ivan Kovbasniuk (cla). 64 Dreamstime.com: Mohammed Anwarul Kabir Choudhury (crb)

Cover images: Front: 123RF.com: andreykuzmin tl/ (Compass), madllen clb/ (Sprout), phive2015 tc, rustyphil, Peter Schenk / pschenk fcrb; Alamy Stock Photo: Jupiterimages cla/ (Shuttle); Dorling Kindersley: Andy Crawford tl, Natural History Museum, London crb/ (Blue butterfly), crb/ (Blue night butterfly), crb/ (Purple butterfly), crb/ (Moon Moth), Space and Rocket Center, Alabama cr; Dreamstime.com: Astrofireball t/ (Moon x7), Leonello Calvetti fbl, Torian Dixon / Mrincredible c, Sebastian Kaulitzki / Eraxion cra, Sergey Kichigin / Kichigin crb/ (Snowflake), fclb, Newlight crb, Elena Schweitzer / Egal clb/ (Microscope), Shishkin cla, Vtorous / VaS (Shapes x5); Fotolia: Auris fcra, fcl, dundanim clb/ (Earth), valdis torms cra/ (Atom); Getty Images: MirageC clb; Back: 123RF.com: gradts tc, madllen cb/ (Sprout), phive2015 tl, rustyphil, Peter Schenk / pschenk cr; Alamy Stock Photo: Jupiterimages cla; Dorling Kindersley: Andy Crawford tl/ (Hubble), Space and Rocket Center, Alabama ftl; Dreamstime.com: Torian Dixon / Mrincredible crb, Sebastian Kaulitzki / Eraxion cra, Sergey Kichigin / Kichigin fclb, Newlight crb/ (Scale), Elena Schweitzer / Egal clb, Shishkin cb, Vtorous / VaS (Shapes x5); Fotolia: Auris fbl, fcl, dundanim tr; Getty Images: MirageC cb/ (Eyewear); Spine: 123RF.com: phive2015 t

For further information see: www.dkimages.com

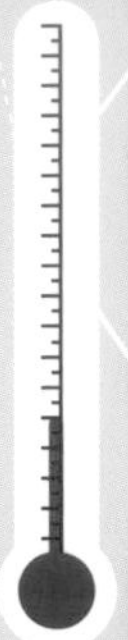

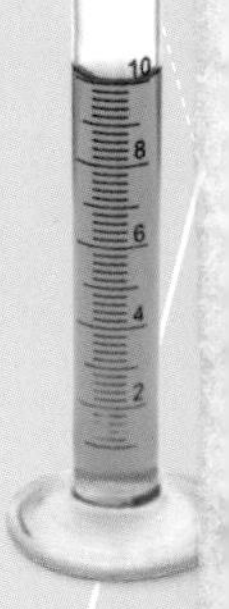

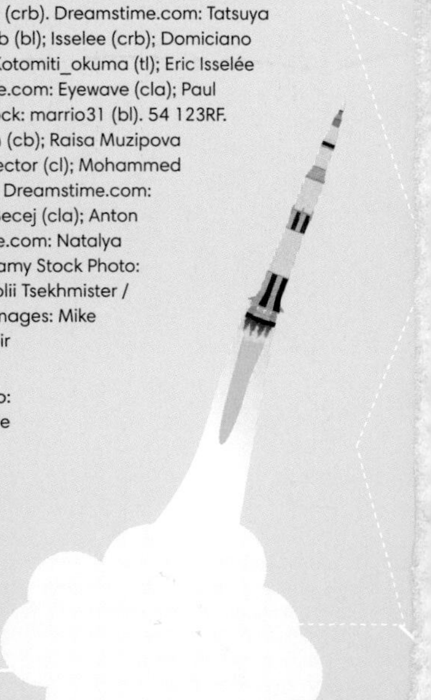